RECENT DEVELOPMENTS IN VIDEO SURVEILLANCE

Edited by **Hazem El-Alfy**

Recent Developments in Video Surveillance
Edited by Hazem El-Alfy

Published by InTech
Janeza Trdine 9, 51000 Rijeka, Croatia

Publishing Process Manager Marija Radja

Technical Editor Teodora Smiljanic

Cover Designer InTech Design Team

Additional hard copies can be obtained from orders@intechopen.com

Recent Developments in Video Surveillance, Edited by Hazem El-Alfy
p. cm.
ISBN 978-953-51-0468-1

For EU product safety concerns:
IN TECH d.o.o., Prolaz Marije Krucifikse Kozulić 3, 51000 Rijeka, Croatia,
info@intechopen.com or visit our website at intechopen.com.

Meet the editor

Dr. Hazem El-Alfy is an Assistant Professor at the University of Alexandria, Egypt. He graduated with honors from the Department of Computer Science at the University of Alexandria in 1997 and later received a Masters degree in Engineering Mathematics in 2001 from the same university. He then worked as a Research Assistant at the University of Maryland at College Park where he earned another Masters degree in 2005 and a doctoral degree in 2009, both from the Computer Science Department. His research interests are in video processing and multi-camera management with applications in surveillance and robot path planning. He has publications in top international conferences on Robotics, Multimedia and Artificial Intelligence. Dr. El-Alfy received several awards, honors and research grants from the Faculty of Engineering at Alexandria University.

Contents

Preface IX

Chapter 1 **Compressive Sensing in Visual Tracking 3**
Garrett Warnell and Rama Chellappa

Chapter 2 **A Construction Method for Automatic Human Tracking System with Mobile Agent Technology 17**
Hiroto Kakiuchi, Kozo Tanigawa, Takao Kawamura and Kazunori Sugahara

Chapter 3 **Appearance-Based Retrieval for Tracked Objects in Surveillance Videos 39**
Thi-Lan Le, Monique Thonnat and Alain Boucher

Chapter 4 **Quality Assessment in Video Surveillance 57**
Mikołaj Leszczuk, Piotr Romaniak and Lucjan Janowski

Chapter 5 **Intelligent Surveillance System Based on Stereo Vision for Level Crossings Safety Applications 75**
Nizar Fakhfakh, Louahdi Khoudour, Jean-Luc Bruyelle and El-Miloudi El-Koursi

Chapter 6 **Behavior Recognition Using any Feature Space Representation of Motion Trajectories 101**
Shehzad Khalid

Preface

Surveillance systems have become an essential part in most establishments nowadays. There are many uses to these systems in national security, safety in public areas, flow control in crowded scenes, private safety and in providing special care for the aged and disabled. At the heart of any surveillance system are video cameras which have had their numbers significantly multiply over the last decade, thanks to advances in digital networks and automated video processing. This has resulted in an abundance of available surveillance video which made the process of monitoring them by human operators not only outdated but also practically infeasible. Several methods have been developed to automate the detection and reporting of scenes, events and subjects that satisfy application specific requirements.

The purpose of this book is to collect recent advances in select areas of video surveillance. Research in that area usually combines results from machine learning, artificial intelligence, software engineering, stochastic modeling, signal processing in addition to pattern recognition and digital image/video processing. Solving problems related to video surveillance often requires the reconciliation between several contradicting objectives. This makes it a challenging task and also an open research area where novel solutions are continually presented to overcome earlier shortcomings but still without reaching a final solution.

The book is organized into six chapters outlined as follows:

Chapter 1 addresses the challenges that face surveillance applications due to the increased availability of visual data to be processed. As a case study, the problem of visual tracking is presented, its classical techniques are described and the difficulties that these techniques have to deal with due to increased visual data are illustrated. The emerging theory of compressive sensing is then introduced as a solution to these challenges, applying it to the successive stages of object tracking. Unlike the mathematical oriented approach used earlier, ***Chapter 2*** presents a software engineering approach to the problem of tracking. In particular, the technology of mobile agents is applied to the problem of tracking objects as they move between the fields of view of several cameras. The challenge here is to recover and maintain the identities of targets lost by the system. Neighborhood node determination techniques are introduced, analyzed and compared.

Chapter 3 surveys most recent advances in the area of indexing surveillance video. The challenges in the retrieval of tracked objects from video are presented. Then, existing and suggested solutions are evaluated. This brings us to an important aspect of video surveillance: the difficulty in comparing and evaluating results due to the lack of standards. Subjective assessment of the quality of surveillance video is yet another emerging area presented in this book and is the topic of ***Chapter 4***. It is compared to earlier qualitative assessment approaches such as "user satisfaction" or other quantitative measures of quality deterioration versus frame per second rates. In contrast, the suggested assessment method focuses on recognition and discrimination tasks which fit video surveillance needs more adequately.

Chapter 5 presents an important application of video surveillance in the area of public safety, namely at railroad crossings. Current safety settings include sensor triggered devices that detect objects crossing rail tracks when a train is approaching (danger zone). The suggested approach, however, uses stereo color surveillance cameras to accurately detect, in 3D, obstacles that are either moving or stopped in the danger zone. A novel background subtraction technique that uses color information is developed and, in addition, the chapter contains a clear presentation of a wealth of classical topics in computer vision, such as stereo matching, segmentation and tracking. The book concludes in ***Chapter 6*** with an application in event understanding (event modeling) which lies at the edge between machine learning and computer vision. It highlights the common challenge within the computer vision community of choosing an appropriate data representation. A suitable representation results in more efficient and accurate data processing. This is illustrated in the chapter using a feature space representation for motion trajectories. Clustering of trajectories is then performed more efficiently and is used to detect outliers which are typically reported as suspicious activity.

The chapters of this book comprise multiple areas of video surveillance ranging from classical computer vision areas of video segmentation, stereo matching, anomaly detection and video indexing to recently emerging areas such as quality assessment and compressive sensing. Recent developments in those areas are presented along with practical real life applications. Still, each chapter contains a clear presentation of the area it covers with references to earlier related work. This makes the book available for a wide range of readers. Academic researchers will find a reliable compilation of relevant literature in addition to timely pointers to current advances in the field of video surveillance. Industry practitioners will find useful hints about state-of-the-art applications. The book also provides directions for open problems where further advances can be pursued.

Acknowledgements

I am indebted to many people who assisted me in the different processing stages of this book. In particular, I would like to acknowledge the editorial staff for their professionalism and patience. I also extend special thanks to Behjat Siddiquie, PhD

(Computer Scientist at SRI International, USA) and Vlad I. Morariu, PhD (Research Associate at the University of Maryland, USA) for reviewing several chapters and providing helpful comments.

April 2012

Hazem El-Alfy
Dept. of Engineering Mathematics and Physics
Faculty of Engineering, Alexandria University
Alexandria,
EGYPT

1

Compressive Sensing in Visual Tracking

Garrett Warnell and Rama Chellappa
University of Maryland, College Park
USA

1. Introduction

Visual tracking is an important component of many video surveillance systems. Specifically, visual tracking refers to the inference of physical object properties (e.g., spatial position or velocity) from video data. This is a well-established problem that has received a great deal of attention from the research community (see, e.g., the survey (Yilmaz et al., 2006)). Classical techniques often involve performing object segmentation, feature extraction, and sequential estimation for the quantities of interest.

Recently, a new challenge has emerged in this field. Tracking has become increasingly difficult due to the growing availability of cheap, high-quality visual sensors. The issue is data deluge (Baraniuk, 2011), i.e., the quantity of data prohibits its usefulness due to the inability of the system to efficiently process it. For example, a video surveillance system consisting of many high-definition cameras may be able to gather data at a high rate (perhaps gigabytes per second), but may not be able to process, store, or transmit the acquired video data under real-time and bandwidth constraints.

The emerging theory of *compressive sensing (CS)* has the potential to address this problem. Under certain conditions related to sparse representations, it effectively reduces the amount of data collected by the system while retaining the ability to faithfully reconstruct the information of interest. Using novel sensors based on this theory, there is hope to accomplish tracking tasks while collecting significantly less data than traditional systems.

This chapter will first present classical components of and approaches to visual tracking, including background subtraction, the Kalman and particle filters, and the mean shift tracker. This will be followed by an overview of CS, especially as it relates to imaging. The rest of the chapter will focus on several recent works that demonstrate the use and benefit of CS in visual tracking.

2. Classical visual tracking

The purpose of this section is to give an overview of classical visual tracking. As a popular component present in many methods, an overview of techniques used for background subtraction will be provided. Next, the focus will shift to the probabilistic tracking frameworks that define the Kalman and particle filters. This will be followed by a presentation of an effective application-specific method: the mean shift tracker.

2.1 Background subtraction

An important first step in many visual tracking systems is the extraction of regions of interest (e.g, those containing objects) from the rest of the scene. These regions are collectively termed the *foreground*, and the technique of *background subtraction* aims to segment it from the background (i.e., the rest of the frame). Once the foreground has been identified, the task of feature extraction becomes much easier due to the resulting decrease in data.

2.1.1 Hypothesis testing formulation

When dealing with digital images, one can pose the problem of background subtraction as a hypothesis test (Poor, 1994; Sankaranarayanan et al., 2008) for each pixel in the image. The null hypothesis (H_0) is that a pixel belongs to the background, while the alternate hypothesis (H_1) is that it belongs to the foreground. Let p denote the measurement observed at an arbitrary pixel. The form of p varies with the sensing modality, however its most common forms are that of a scalar (e.g., light intensity in a gray scale image) or a three-vector (e.g., a color triple in a color image). Whatever they physically represent, let F_B denote the probability distribution over the possible values of p when the pixel belongs to the background, and F_T the distribution for pixels in the foreground. The hypothesis test formulation of background subtraction can then be written as:

$$\begin{aligned} H_0 : \quad & p \sim F_B \\ H_1 : \quad & p \sim F_T \end{aligned} \tag{2.1}$$

The optimal Bayes decision rule for (2.1) is given by:

$$\frac{f_B(p)}{f_T(p)} \underset{H_1}{\overset{H_0}{\gtrless}} \tau \tag{2.2}$$

where $f_B(p)$ and $f_T(p)$ denote the densities corresponding to F_B and F_T respectively, and τ is a threshold determined by the Bayes risk. It is often the case, however, that very little is known about the foreground, and thus the form of F_T. One way of handling this is to assume F_T to be the uniform distribution over the possible values of p. In this case, the above reduces to:

$$f_B(p) \underset{H_1}{\overset{H_0}{\gtrless}} \theta \tag{2.3}$$

where θ is dependent on τ the range of p.

In practice, the optimum value of θ is typically unknown. Therefore, θ is often chosen in an *ad-hoc* fashion such that the decision rule gives pleasing results for the data of interest.

2.1.2 A simple background model

It will now be useful to introduce some notation to handle the temporal and spatial dimensions intrinsic to video data. Let p_i^t denote the value of the ith pixel in the tth frame. Further, let B_i^t parametrize the corresponding background distribution, denoted $F_{B,i,t}$, which may vary with respect to both time and space. In order to select a good hypothesis test, the focus of the background subtraction problem is on how to determine B_i^t from the available data.

An intuitive, albeit naive, approach to this problem is to presume a static background model with respect to time. A common form of this assumption is that $F_{B,i,t}$ is Gaussian with the same covariance for all i. Such a distribution is parametrized only by its mean, and let μ_i specify this value. Substituting the Gaussian density function for $f_B(p)$ in (2.3) yields the following decision rule:

$$\|p_i^t - \mu_i\|_2 \underset{H_1}{\overset{H_0}{\lessgtr}} \eta \quad (2.4)$$

for some threshold η dependent on θ and the covariance. In essence, the above rule amounts to a simple thresholding of the background likelihood function evaluated at the pixel value of interest. This is an intuitive way to perform background subtraction in that if the difference between the background μ_i and the observation p_i^t is high enough, the pixel is classified as belonging to the foreground. Further, this method is computationally advantageous in that it simply requires storing a background image, μ_i for all i, and thresholding the difference between it and a test image. An example of this method is shown in Figure 1.

Fig. 1. Background subtraction results for the static unimodal Gaussian model. Left: static background image. Middle: image with human. Right: background subtraction results using the method in (2.4)

2.1.3 Dynamic background modeling

The static approach outlined above is simple, but suffers from the inability to cope with a dynamic background. Such a background is common in video due to illumination shifts, camera and object motion, and other changes in the environment. For example, a tree in the background may sway in the breeze, causing pixel measurements to change significantly from one frame to the next (e.g. tree to sky). However, each shift should not cause the pixel to be classified as foreground, which will occur under the unimodal Gaussian model. A solution to this problem is to use *kernel density estimation (KDE)* (Elgammal et al., 2002; Stauffer & Grimson, 1999) to estimate $f_{B,i,t}$ from past data, i.e.

$$f_{B,i,t}(p) = \frac{1}{N} \sum_{j=t-N}^{t-1} K_j(p) \quad (2.5)$$

where K_j is a kernel density function dependent on the observation p_i^j. For example, K_j may be defined as a Gaussian with fixed covariance and mean p_i^j. Using this definition, B_i^t can be thought of as the pixel history $\{p_i^j\}_{j=t-N}^{t-1}$, and $F_{B,i,t}$ becomes a mixture of Gaussians. This method is also adaptive to temporally recent changes in the background, as only the previous N observations are used in the density estimate.

2.2 Tracking

In general, *tracking* is the sequential estimation of a random variable based on observations over which it exerts influence. In the field of video surveillance, this random variable represents certain physical qualities belonging to objects of interest. For example, Broida and Chellappa (Broida & Chellappa, 1986) characterize a two-dimensional object in the image plane via its center of mass and translational velocity. They also incorporate other quantities to capture shape, global scale, and rotational motion. The time sequential estimates of such quantities are referred to as *tracks*.

To facilitate subsequent discussion, it is useful to consider the discrete time state space representation of the overall system that encompasses object motion and observation. The *state* of the system represents the unknown values of interest (e.g., object position), and in this section it will be denoted by a *state vector*, $\mathbf{x}_t$, whose components correspond to these quantities. Observations of the system will be denoted by $\mathbf{y}_t$, and are obtained via a mapping from the image to the observation space. This process is referred to as *feature extraction*, which will not be the focus of this chapter. Instead, it is assumed that observations are provided to the tracker with some specified probabilistic relationship between observation and state. Given the complicated nature of feature extraction, it is often the case that this relationship is heuristically selected based on some intuition regarding the feature extraction process.

In the context of the above discussion, the goal of a tracker is to provide sequential estimates of $\mathbf{x}_t$ using the observations $(\mathbf{y}_0, \ldots, \mathbf{y}_t)$. In the following sections, a few prominent methods by which this is done will be considered.

2.2.1 Kalman filtering

The Kalman filter is a recursive tracking technique that is widely popular due to its computational efficiency and ease of implementation. Under specific system assumptions, it is able to provide a state estimate that is optimal according to a few popular metrics. This section will outline these assumptions and detail the Kalman filtering method that is used to compute the sequential state estimates.

Specifically, the assumptions that yield optimality are that the physical process governing the behavior of the state should be linear and affected by additive white Gaussian *process noise*, $\mathbf{w}_t$, i.e. (Anderson & Moore, 1979),

$$\begin{aligned} \mathbf{x}_{t+1} &= \mathbf{F}_t \mathbf{x}_t + \mathbf{w}_t \\ \mathbf{w}_t &\sim \mathcal{N}(\mathbf{0}, \mathbf{Q}_t), \ \mathbb{E}\left[\mathbf{w}_k \mathbf{w}_l^T\right] = \mathbf{Q}_k \delta_{kl} \quad , \end{aligned} \tag{2.6}$$

where δ_{kl} is equal to one when $k = l$, and is zero otherwise. The process noise allows for the model to remain valid even when the relationship between $\mathbf{x}_{t+1}$ and $\mathbf{x}_t$ is not completely captured by $\mathbf{F}_t$.

The required relationship between $\mathbf{y}_t$ and $\mathbf{x}_t$ is specified by:

$$\mathbf{y}_t = \mathbf{H}_t^T \mathbf{x}_t + \mathbf{v}_t \tag{2.7}$$

$$\mathbf{v}_t \sim \mathcal{N}(\mathbf{0}, \mathbf{R}_t), \ \mathbb{E}\left[\mathbf{v}_k \mathbf{v}_l^T\right] = \mathbf{R}_k \delta_{kl} \quad .$$

Notice that, just as in the state model, the relationship between the observation and the state is assumed to be linear and affected by white Gaussian noise $\mathbf{v}_t$. This is referred to as *measurement noise*, and is assumed to be independent of $\{\mathbf{w}_t\}_{t=0}^{\infty}$.

With the above assumptions, the goal of the Kalman filter is to compute the best estimate of $\mathbf{x}_k$ from the observations $(\mathbf{y}_0, \ldots, \mathbf{y}_t)$. What is meant by "best" can vary from application to application, but common criterion yield the *maximum a posteriori (MAP)* and *minimum mean squared error (MMSE)* estimators. Regardless of the estimator chosen, the value it yields can be computed using the posterior density $p(\mathbf{x}_t|\mathbf{y}_0, \ldots, \mathbf{y}_t)$. For example, the MMSE estimate is the mean of this density and the MAP estimate is the value of $\mathbf{x}_t$ that maximizes it.

Under the assumptions made when specifying the state and observation equations, the MMSE and MAP estimates are identical. Since successive estimates can be calculated recursively, the Kalman filter provides this estimate without having to re-compute $p(\mathbf{x}_t|\mathbf{y}_0, \ldots, \mathbf{y}_t)$ each time a new observation is received. This benefit requires the additional assumption that $\mathbf{x}_0 \sim \mathcal{N}(\bar{\mathbf{x}}_0, \mathbf{P}_0)$, which is equivalent to assuming $\mathbf{x}_0$ and $\mathbf{y}_0$ to be jointly Gaussian, i.e.,

$$\begin{bmatrix} \mathbf{x}_0 \\ \mathbf{y}_0 \end{bmatrix} \sim \mathcal{N}\left(\begin{bmatrix} \bar{\mathbf{x}}_0 \\ \mathbf{H}_0^T \bar{\mathbf{x}}_0 \end{bmatrix}, \begin{bmatrix} \mathbf{P}_0 & \mathbf{P}_0 \mathbf{H}_0 \\ \mathbf{H}_0^T \mathbf{P}_0 & \mathbf{H}_0^T \mathbf{P}_0 \mathbf{H}_0 + \mathbf{R}_0 \end{bmatrix} \right) \quad , \tag{2.8}$$

which yields

$$\mathbf{x}_0|\mathbf{y}_0 \sim \mathcal{N}\left(\hat{\mathbf{x}}_{0|0}, \mathbf{\Sigma}_{0|0}\right) \tag{2.9}$$

$$\hat{\mathbf{x}}_{0|0} = \bar{\mathbf{x}}_0 + \mathbf{P}_0 \mathbf{H}_0 (\mathbf{H}_0^T \mathbf{P}_0 \mathbf{H}_0 + \mathbf{R}_0)^{-1} (\mathbf{y}_0 - \mathbf{H}_0^T \bar{\mathbf{x}}_0)$$

$$\mathbf{\Sigma}_{0|0} = \mathbf{P}_0 - \mathbf{P}_0 \mathbf{H}_0 (\mathbf{H}_0^T \mathbf{P}_0 \mathbf{H}_0 + \mathbf{R}_0)^{-1} \mathbf{H}_0^T \mathbf{P}_0 \quad . \tag{2.10}$$

Since $\mathbf{x}_0|\mathbf{y}_0$ is Gaussian, both its MMSE and MAP estimates are given by the mean of this distribution, i.e., $\hat{\mathbf{x}}_{0|0}$. The subscript indicates that this is the estimate of $\mathbf{x}_0$ given observations up to time 0.

From this starting point, the Kalman filter calculates subsequent estimates ($\hat{\mathbf{x}}_{t|t}$ in general) using a two step procedure. First, it can be seen that $\mathbf{x}_{t+1}|\mathbf{y}_{0:t}$ is also Gaussian, with mean and covariance given by

$$\hat{\mathbf{x}}_{t+1|t} = \mathbf{F}_t \hat{\mathbf{x}}_{t|t} \tag{2.11}$$

$$\mathbf{\Sigma}_{t+1|t} = \mathbf{F}_t \mathbf{\Sigma}_{t|t} \mathbf{F}_t^T + \mathbf{Q}_t \quad .$$

The above are known as the *time update equations*. Once $\mathbf{y}_{t+1}$ is observed, the second step of the Kalman filter is to adjust the prediction $\hat{\mathbf{x}}_{t+1|t}$ to one that incorporates the information provided by the new observation. This is done via the *measurement update equations*:

$$\hat{\mathbf{x}}_{t+1|t+1} = \hat{\mathbf{x}}_{t+1|t} + \boldsymbol{\Sigma}_{t+1|t}\mathbf{H}_{t+1}(\mathbf{H}_{t+1}^T\boldsymbol{\Sigma}_{t+1|t}\mathbf{H}_{t+1} + \mathbf{R}_{t+1})^{-1}(\mathbf{y}_{t+1} - \mathbf{H}_{t+1}^T\hat{\mathbf{x}}_{t+1|t}) \quad (2.12)$$

$$\boldsymbol{\Sigma}_{t+1|t+1} = \boldsymbol{\Sigma}_{t+1|t} - \boldsymbol{\Sigma}_{t+1|t}\mathbf{H}_{t+1}(\mathbf{H}_{t+1}^T\boldsymbol{\Sigma}_{t+1|t}\mathbf{H}_{t+1} + \mathbf{R}_{t+1})^{-1}\mathbf{H}_{t+1}^T\boldsymbol{\Sigma}_{t+1|t} \quad . \quad (2.13)$$

Using the above steps at each time instant, the Kalman filter provides optimal tracks $\{\hat{\mathbf{x}}_{t|t}\}_{t=0}^{\infty}$ that are calculated in a recursive and efficient manner. The optimality of the estimates comes at the cost of requiring the assumptions of linearity and Gaussianity in the state space formulation of the system. Even without the Gaussian assumptions, the filter is optimal among the class of linear filters.

2.2.2 Particle filtering

Since it is able to operate in an unconstrained setting, the *particle filter* (Doucet et al., 2001; Isard & Blake, 1996) is a more general approach to sequential estimation. However, this expanded utility comes at the cost of high computational complexity. The particle filter is a *sequential Monte Carlo method*, using samples of the conditional distribution in order to approximate it and thus the desired estimates. There are many variations of the particle filter, but the focus of this section shall be on the so-called *bootstrap filter*.

Assume the system of interest behaves according to the following known densities:

$$p(\mathbf{x}_0) \quad , \quad (2.14)$$

$$p(\mathbf{x}_t|\mathbf{x}_{t-1}), \quad t \geq 1 \quad , \text{and} \quad (2.15)$$

$$p(\mathbf{y}_t|\mathbf{x}_t), \quad t \geq 1 \quad . \quad (2.16)$$

Note that the more general specifications $p(\mathbf{x}_t|\mathbf{x}_{t-1})$ and $p(\mathbf{y}_t|\mathbf{x}_t)$ replace the linear, Gaussian descriptions of the system and observation behaviors necessary for the Kalman filter. In order to achieve the goal of tracking, it is necessary to have some information regarding $p(\mathbf{x}_{0:t}|\mathbf{y}_{1:t})$ (from which $p(\mathbf{x}_t|\mathbf{y}_{1:t})$ is apparent), where $\mathbf{x}_{0:t} = (\mathbf{x}_0, \ldots, \mathbf{x}_t)$, and similarly for $\mathbf{y}_{1:t}$. Here, we depart from the previous notation and assume that the first observation is available at $t = 1$.

In a purely Bayesian sense, one could compute the conditional density as

$$p(\mathbf{x}_{0:t}|\mathbf{y}_{1:t}) = \frac{p(\mathbf{y}_{1:t}|\mathbf{x}_{0:t})p(\mathbf{x}_{0:t})}{\int p(\mathbf{y}_{1:t}|\mathbf{x}_{0:t})p(\mathbf{x}_{0:t})d\mathbf{x}_{0:t}} \quad , \quad (2.17)$$

which leads to a recursive formula

$$p(\mathbf{x}_{0:t}|\mathbf{y}_{1:t}) = p(\mathbf{x}_{0:t-1}|\mathbf{y}_{1:t-1})\frac{p(\mathbf{y}_t|\mathbf{x}_t)p(\mathbf{x}_t|\mathbf{x}_{t-1})}{p(\mathbf{y}_t|\mathbf{y}_{t-1})} \quad . \quad (2.18)$$

A similar type of recursion can be shown to exist for the marginal density $p(\mathbf{x}_t|\mathbf{y}_{1:t})$. While the above expressions seem simple, for general distributions in (2.14) (2.15) and (2.16), they often become prohibitively difficult to evaluate due to analytic and computational complexity.

The particle filter avoids the analytic difficulties above using Monte Carlo sampling. If N i.i.d. *particles* (samples), $\{\mathbf{x}_{0:t}^{(i)}\}_{i=1}^{N}$, drawn from $p(\mathbf{x}_{0:t}|\mathbf{y}_{1:t})$ were available, one could approximate the density by placing a Dirac delta mass at the location of each sample, i.e.,

$$p(\mathbf{x}_{0:t}|\mathbf{y}_{1:t}) \approx P_N(\mathbf{x}_{0:t}|\mathbf{y}_{1:t}) = \frac{1}{N}\sum_{i=1}^{N} \delta(\mathbf{x}_{0:t} - \mathbf{x}_{0:t}^{(i)}) \quad . \tag{2.19}$$

It would then be straightforward to use P_N to calculate an estimate of the random variable (i.e. a track). However, this method presents its own difficulty in that it is usually impractical to obtain the samples $\{\mathbf{x}_{0:t}^{(i)}\}_{i=1}^{N}$.

The bootstrap filter is based on a technique called *sequential importance sampling*, which is used to overcome the issue above. Samples are initially drawn from the known prior distribution $p(\mathbf{x}_0)$, from which it is straightforward to generate samples $\{\mathbf{x}_0^{(i)}\}_{i=1}^{N}$. Next, importance sampling occurs. First, a prediction step takes place, generating candidate samples $\{\tilde{\mathbf{x}}_1^{(i)}\}_{i=1}^{N}$ by drawing $\tilde{\mathbf{x}}_1^{(i)}$ from $p(\mathbf{x}_1|\mathbf{x}_0^{(i)})$ for each i. From here, *importance weights* $\tilde{w}_1^{(i)} = p(\mathbf{y}_1|\tilde{\mathbf{x}}_1^{(i)})$ are calculated based on the observation $\mathbf{y}_1$ and adjusted such that they are normalized (i.e. such that $\sum_i \tilde{w}_1^{(i)} = 1$). The filter then enters the selection step, where samples $\{\mathbf{x}_1^{(i)}\}_{i=1}^{N}$ are generated via draws from a discrete distribution over $\{\tilde{\mathbf{x}}_1^{(i)}\}_{i=1}^{N}$ with the probability for the ith element given by $\tilde{w}_1^{(i)}$. This process is then repeated to obtain $\{\mathbf{x}_2^{(i)}\}_{i=1}^{N}$ from $\{\mathbf{x}_1^{(i)}\}_{i=1}^{N}$ and $\mathbf{y}_2$, and so forth.

Due to the selection step, those candidate particles $\tilde{\mathbf{x}}_t^{(i)}$ for which $p(\mathbf{y}_t|\tilde{\mathbf{x}}_t^{i})$ is low will not propagate to the next stage. The samples that survive are those that explain the data well, and are thus concentrated in the most dense areas of $p(\mathbf{x}_t|\mathbf{y}_{1:t})$. Therefore, the computed value for common estimators such as the mean and mode will be good approximations of their actual values. Further, note that the candidate particles are drawn from $p(\mathbf{x}_t|\mathbf{x}_{t-1})$, which introduces process noise to prevent the particles from becoming too short-sighted.

Using the estimate calculated from the density approximation yielded by the particles $\{\mathbf{x}_t^{(i)}\}_{i=1}^{N}$, the particle filter is able provide tracks that are optimal for a wide variety of criteria in a more general setting than that required by the Kalman filter. However, the validity of the track depends on the ability of the particles to sufficiently characterize the underlying density. Often, this may require a large number of particles, which can lead to a high computational cost.

2.2.3 Mean shift tracking

Unlike the Kalman and particle filters, the *mean shift* tracker (Comaniciu et al., 2003) is a procedure designed specifically for visual data. The feature employed, a spatially weighted color histogram, is computed directly from the input images. The estimate for the object position in the image plane is defined as the mode of a density over spatial locations, where this density is defined using a similarity measure between the histogram for an object model (i.e. a "template") and the histogram at a location of interest. The mean shift procedure (Comaniciu & Meer, 2002) is then used to find this mode.

In general, the mean shift procedure provides a way to perform gradient ascent on an unknown density using only samples generated by this density. It achieves this via selecting a specific method of density estimation and analytically deriving a data-dependent term that corresponds to the gradient of the estimate. This term is known as the mean shift, and it can be used as the step term in a mode-seeking gradient ascent procedure. Specifically, non-parametric KDE is employed, i.e.,

$$\hat{f}(\mathbf{x}) = \frac{1}{nh^d} \sum_{i=1}^{n} K\left(\frac{\mathbf{x}-\mathbf{x}_i}{h}\right) \quad , \tag{2.20}$$

where the d-dimensional vector $\mathbf{x}$ represents the feature, $\hat{f}(\cdot)$ the estimated density, and $K(\cdot)$ a *kernel function*. The kernel function is assumed to be radially symmetric, i.e., $K(\mathbf{x}) = c_{k,d}k(\|\mathbf{x}\|^2)$ for some function $k(\cdot)$ and normalizing constant $c_{k,d}$. Using this in (2.20), $\hat{f}(\mathbf{x})$ becomes

$$\hat{f}_{h,K}(\mathbf{x}) = \frac{c_{k,d}}{nh^d} \sum_{i=1}^{n} k(\|\frac{\mathbf{x}-\mathbf{x}_i}{h}\|^2) \quad . \tag{2.21}$$

Ultimately, it is the gradient of this approximation, $\nabla \hat{f}_{h,K}$, that is of interest. Letting $g(\cdot) = -k'(\cdot)$, it is given by

$$\nabla \hat{f}_{h,K}(\mathbf{x}) = \frac{2c_{k,d}}{nh^{d+2}} \left[\sum_{i=1}^{n} g\left(\|\frac{\mathbf{x}-\mathbf{x}_i}{h}\|^2\right)\right] \left[\frac{\sum_{i=1}^{n} \mathbf{x}_i g\left(\|\frac{\mathbf{x}-\mathbf{x}_i}{h}\|^2\right)}{\sum_{i=1}^{n} g\left(\|\frac{\mathbf{x}-\mathbf{x}_i}{h}\|^2\right)} - \mathbf{x}\right] \quad . \tag{2.22}$$

Using $g(\cdot)$ to define a new kernel $G(\mathbf{x}) = c_{g,d}g(\|\mathbf{x}\|^2)$, (2.22) can be rewritten as

$$\nabla \hat{f}_{h,K}(\mathbf{x}) = \frac{2c_{k,d}}{n^2 c_{g,d}} \hat{f}_{h,G}(\mathbf{x}) \mathbf{m}_{h,G}(\mathbf{x}) \quad , \tag{2.23}$$

where $\mathbf{m}_{h,G}(\mathbf{x})$ denotes the mean shift:

$$\mathbf{m}_{h,G}(\mathbf{x}) = \left[\frac{\sum_{i=1}^{n} \mathbf{x}_i g\left(\|\frac{\mathbf{x}-\mathbf{x}_i}{h}\|^2\right)}{\sum_{i=1}^{n} g\left(\|\frac{\mathbf{x}-\mathbf{x}_i}{h}\|^2\right)} - \mathbf{x}\right] \quad . \tag{2.24}$$

It can be seen from (2.23) that $\mathbf{m}_{h,G}(\mathbf{x})$ is proportional to $\nabla \hat{f}_{h,K}(\mathbf{x})$, and thus may be used as a step direction in a gradient ascent procedure to find a maximum of $\hat{f}_{h,K}(\mathbf{x})$ (i.e., a mode).

(Comaniciu et al., 2003) utilize the above procedure when tracking objects in the image plane. The selected feature is a spatially weighted color histogram computed over a normalized window of finite spatial support. The spatial weighting is defined by an isotropic kernel $k(\cdot)$, and the object model is given by an m-bin histogram $\hat{\mathbf{q}} = \{\hat{q}_u\}_{u=1}^{m}$, where

$$\hat{q}_u = C \sum_{i=1}^{n} k(\|\mathbf{x}_i^*\|^2) \delta\left[b(\mathbf{x}_i^*) - u\right] \quad . \tag{2.25}$$

$\mathbf{x}_i^*$ denotes the spatial location of the ith pixel in the n pixel window containing the object model, assuming the center of the window to be located at $\mathbf{0}$. $\delta\left[b(\mathbf{x}_i^* - u\right]$ is 1 when the pixel value at $\mathbf{x}_i^*$ falls into the uth bin of the histogram, and 0 otherwise. Finally, C is a normalizing constant to ensure that $\mathbf{q}$ is a true histogram.

An object candidate feature located at position $\mathbf{y}$ is denoted by $\hat{\mathbf{p}}(\mathbf{y})$, and is calculated in a manner similar to $\hat{\mathbf{q}}$, except $k(\|\mathbf{x}_i^*\|^2)$ is replaced by $k(\|\mathbf{y} - \mathbf{x}_i\|^2)$ to account for the new window location.

To capture a notion of similarity between $\hat{\mathbf{p}}(\mathbf{y})$ and $\hat{\mathbf{q}}$, the Bhattacharyya coefficient is used, i.e.,

$$d(\mathbf{y}) = \sqrt{1 - \hat{\rho}(\mathbf{y})} \quad , \tag{2.26}$$

where $\hat{\rho}(\mathbf{y}) = \sum_{u=1}^{m} \sqrt{\hat{p}_u(\mathbf{y})\hat{q}_u}$ is the Bhattacharyya coefficient.

An approximation of $\hat{\rho}(\mathbf{y})$ is provided by

$$\hat{\rho}(\mathbf{y}) = \frac{1}{2}\sum_{u=1}^{m} \sqrt{\hat{p}_u(\mathbf{y}_0)\hat{q}_u} + \frac{C_h}{2}\sum_{i=1}^{n} w_i k\left(\|\frac{\mathbf{y} - \mathbf{x}_i}{h}\|^2\right) \quad . \tag{2.27}$$

Above, $\mathbf{y}_0$ represents an initial location provided by the track from the previous frame. The weights $\{w_i\}_{i=1}^{n}$ are calculated as a function of $\hat{\mathbf{q}}$, $\hat{\mathbf{p}}(\mathbf{y}_0)$, and $b(\mathbf{x}_i)$. To minimize the distance in (2.26), the second term of (2.27) should be maximized with respect to $\mathbf{y}$. This term can be interpreted as a nonparametric weighted KDE with kernel function $k(\cdot)$. Thus, the mean shift procedure can be used to iterate over $\mathbf{y}$ and find that value which minimizes $d(\mathbf{y})$. The result is then taken to be the location estimate (track) for the current frame.

2.3 The data challenge

Given the above background, it can be seen how large amounts of data can be of detriment to tracking. Background subtraction techniques may require complicated density estimates for each pixel, which become burdensome in the presence of high-resolution imagery. The filtering methods presented above are not specific to the amount of data, but more of it leads to greater computational complexity when performing the estimation. Likewise, higher data dimensionality is of detriment to mean shift tracking, specifically during the required density estimation and mode search. This extra data could be due to higher sensor resolution or perhaps the presence of multiple sensors (Sankaranarayanan et al., 2008)(Sankaranarayanan & Chellappa, 2008). Therefore, new tracking strategies must be developed. The hope for finding such strategies comes from the fact that there is a substantial difference in the amount of data collected by these systems compared to the quantity of information that is ultimately of use. Compressive sensing provides a new perspective that radically changes the sensing process with the above observation in mind.

3. Compressive sensing

Compressive sensing is an emerging theory that allows for a certain class of discrete signals to be adequately sensed using far fewer measurements than the dimension of the ambient space in which they reside. By "adequately sensed," it is meant that the signal of interest can be accurately inferred from the measurements collected during the sensing process. In the context of imaging, consider an unknown $n \times n$ grayscale image $\mathbf{F}$, i.e., $\mathbf{F} \in \mathbb{R}^{n \times n}$. A traditional camera measures $\mathbf{F}$ using an $n \times n$ array of photodetectors, where the measurement collected at each detector corresponds to a single pixel value in $\mathbf{F}$. If $\mathbf{F}$ is vectorized as $\mathbf{x} \in \mathbb{R}^N$ ($N = n^2$), then the imaging strategy described above amounts to (in the noiseless case) $\hat{\mathbf{x}} = \mathbf{y} = \mathbf{I}\mathbf{x}$ (Romberg, 2008), where $\hat{\mathbf{x}}$ is the inferred value of $\mathbf{x}$ using the measurements $\mathbf{y}$. Each component of $\mathbf{y}$ (i.e., a measurement) corresponds to a single component of $\mathbf{x}$, and this relationship is captured by representing the sensing process as the identity matrix $\mathbf{I}$. Since $\mathbf{x}$ is the quantity of interest, estimating it from $\mathbf{y}$ also amounts to a simple identity mapping, i.e. $\hat{\mathbf{x}}(\mathbf{y}) = \mathbf{y}$. However, both the measurement and estimation process can change, giving rise to interesting and useful signal acquisition methodologies.

For practical purposes, it is often the case that $\mathbf{x}$ is represented using far fewer measurements than the N collected above. For example, using *transform coding* methods (e.g., JPEG 2000), $\mathbf{x}$ can usually be closely approximated by specifying very few values compared to N (Bruckstein et al., 2009). This is accomplished via obtaining $\mathbf{b} = \mathbf{B}\mathbf{x}$ for some orthonormal basis $\mathbf{B}$ (e.g., the wavelet basis), and setting all but the k largest components of $\mathbf{b}$ to zero. If this new vector is denoted $\mathbf{b}_k$, then the transform coding approximation of $\mathbf{x}$ is given by $\hat{\mathbf{x}} = \mathbf{B}^{-1}\mathbf{b}_k$. If $\|\mathbf{x} - \hat{\mathbf{x}}\|_2$ is small, then this approximation is a good one. Since $\mathbf{B}$ is orthonormal, this condition also requires that $\|\mathbf{b} - \mathbf{b}_k\|_2$ be small as well. If such is the case, $\mathbf{b}$ is said to be *k-sparse* (and $\mathbf{x}$ *k-sparse in* $\mathbf{B}$), i.e., most of the energy in $\mathbf{b}$ is distributed among very few of its components. Thus, if the value of $\mathbf{x}$ is known, and $\mathbf{x}$ is k-sparse in $\mathbf{B}$, a good approximation of $\mathbf{x}$ can be obtained from $\mathbf{b}_k$. Compression comes about since $\mathbf{b}_k$ (and thus $\mathbf{x}$) can be specified using just $2k$ quantities instead of N: the values and locations of the k largest coefficients in $\mathbf{b}$. However, extracting such information requires full knowledge of $\mathbf{x}$, which necessitates N measurements using the traditional imaging system above. Thus, N data points must be collected when in essence all but $2k$ are thrown away. This is not completely unjustified, as one cannot hope to form $\mathbf{b}_k$ without knowing $\mathbf{b}$. On the other hand, such a large disparity between the amount of data collected and the amount that is truly useful seems wasteful.

This glaring disparity is what CS seeks to address. Instead of collecting N measurements of $\mathbf{x}$, the CS strategy is to collect M, where $M << N$ and depends on k. As long as $\mathbf{x}$ is k-sparse in some basis and an appropriate decoding procedure is employed, these M values yield a good approximation of $\mathbf{x}$. For example, let $\mathbf{\Phi} \in \mathbb{R}^{M \times N}$ be the *measurement matrix* by which these values, $\mathbf{y} \in \mathbb{R}^M$, are obtained as $\mathbf{y} = \mathbf{\Phi}\mathbf{x}$. Further, assume $\mathbf{x}$ is k-sparse. It is possible to recover $\mathbf{x}$ from $\mathbf{y}$ if $\mathbf{\Phi}$ has the *restricted isometry property (RIP)* of order $2k$ (Candès & Wakin, 2008), i.e., the smallest δ for which

$$(1 - \delta) \leq \frac{\|\mathbf{\Phi}\mathbf{x}\|_2^2}{\|\mathbf{x}\|_2^2} \leq (1 + \delta) \tag{3.1}$$

holds for all $2k$-sparse vectors is not too close to 1. An intuitive interpretation of this property is that it ensures that all $2k$-sparse vectors do not lie in Null($\mathbf{\Phi}$). This guarantees that a unique measurement $\mathbf{y}$ is generated for each k-sparse $\mathbf{x}$ even though $\mathbf{\Phi}$ is underdetermined.

An example $\mathbf{\Phi}$ that satisfies the above conditions is one for which entries are drawn from the Bernoulli distribution over the discrete set $\{\frac{-1}{\sqrt{N}}, \frac{1}{\sqrt{N}}\}$ and each realization is equally likely (Baraniuk, 2007). If, in addition, M is selected such that $M > Ck \log N$ for a specific constant

C, it is overwhelmingly likely that $\mathbf{\Phi}$ will be $2k$-RIP. There are other constructions that provide similar guarantees given slightly different bounds on M, but the concept remains unchanged: if M is "large enough," $\mathbf{\Phi}$ will exhibit the RIP with overwhelming probability. Given such a matrix, and considering that this implies a unique $\mathbf{y}$ for each k-sparse $\mathbf{x}$, an estimate $\hat{\mathbf{x}}$ of $\mathbf{x}$ is ideally calculated from $\mathbf{y}$ as

$$\hat{\mathbf{x}} = \min_{\mathbf{z} \in \mathbb{R}^N} \|\mathbf{z}\|_0 \quad \text{subject to} \quad \mathbf{\Phi z} = \mathbf{y} \quad , \tag{3.2}$$

where $\|\cdot\|_0$, referred to as the ℓ_0 "norm," counts the number of nonzero entries in $\mathbf{z}$. Thus, (3.2) seeks the sparsest vector that explains the observation $\mathbf{y}$. In practice, (3.2) is not very useful since the program it specifies has combinatorial complexity. However, this problem is also mitigated due to the special construction of $\mathbf{\Phi}$ and the fact that $\mathbf{x}$ is k-sparse. Under these conditions, the solution of the following program yields the same results as (3.2) with overwhelming probability:

$$\hat{\mathbf{x}} = \min_{\mathbf{x} \in \mathbb{R}^N} \|\mathbf{z}\|_1 \quad \text{subject to} \quad \mathbf{\Phi z} = \mathbf{y} \quad . \tag{3.3}$$

Thus, by modifying the sensor to use $\mathbf{\Phi}$ and the decoder to use (3.3), $M << N$ measurements of a k-sparse $\mathbf{x}$ suffice to retain the ability to reconstruct it.

Sensors based on the above theory are beginning emerge (Willett et al., 2011). One of the most notable is the single pixel camera (Duarte et al., 2008), where measurements specified by each row of $\mathbf{\Phi}$ are sequentially computed in the optical domain via a digital micromirror device and a single photodiode. Many of the strategies discussed in the following section assume that the tracking system is such that these compressive sensors replace more traditional cameras.

4. Compressive sensing in video surveillance

Compressive sensing can help alleviate some of the challenges associated with performing classical tracking in the presence of overwhelming amounts of data. By replacing traditional cameras with compressive sensors or by making use of CS techniques in other areas of the process, the amount of data that the system must handle can be drastically reduced. However, this capability should not come at the cost of a significant decrease in tracking performance. This section will present a few methods for performing various tracking tasks that take advantage of CS in order to reduce the quantity of data that must be processed. Specifically, recent methods using CS to perform background subtraction, more general signal tracking, multi-view visual tracking, and particle filtering will be discussed.

4.1 Compressive sensing for background subtraction

One of the most intuitive applications of compressive sensing in visual tracking is the modification of background subtraction such that it is able to operate on compressive measurements. As mentioned in Section 2.1, background subtraction aims to segment the object-containing foreground from the uninteresting background. This process not only helps to localize objects, but also reduces the amount of data that must be processed at later stages of tracking. However, traditional background subtraction techniques require that the full image be available before the process can begin. Such a scenario is reminiscent of the problem that

CS aims to address. Noting that the foreground signal (image) is sparse in the spatial domain, (Cevher et al., 2008) have presented a technique via which background subtraction can be performed on compressive measurements of a scene, resulting in a reduced data rate while simultaneously retaining the ability to reconstruct the foreground. More recently, (Warnell et al., 2012) have proposed a modification to this technique which adaptively adjusts the number of compressive measurements collected to the dynamic foreground sparsity typical to surveillance data.

Denote the images comprising a video sequence as $\{\mathbf{x}_t\}_{t=0}^{\infty}$, where $\mathbf{x}_t \in \mathbb{R}^N$ is the vectorized image captured at time t. Cevher et al. model each image as the sum of foreground and background components $\mathbf{f}_t$ and $\mathbf{b}_t$, respectively. That is,

$$\mathbf{x}_t = \mathbf{f}_t + \mathbf{b}_t \quad . \tag{4.1}$$

Assume $\mathbf{x}_t$ is sensed using $\mathbf{\Phi} \in \mathbb{C}^{M \times N}$ to obtain compressive measurements $\mathbf{y}_t = \mathbf{\Phi}\mathbf{x}_t$. If $\Delta(\mathbf{\Phi}, \mathbf{y})$ represents a CS decoding procedure such as (3.3), then the proposed method for estimating $\mathbf{f}_t$ from $\mathbf{y}_t$ is

$$\hat{\mathbf{f}}_t = \Delta(\mathbf{\Phi}, \mathbf{y} - \mathbf{y}_t^b) \quad , \tag{4.2}$$

where it is assumed that $\mathbf{y}_t^b = \mathbf{\Phi}\mathbf{b_t}$ is known via an estimation and update procedure.

To begin, $\mathbf{y}_0^b$ is initialized using a sequence of N compressively sensed background-only frames $\{\mathbf{y}_j^b\}_{j=1}^N$ that appear before the sequence of interest begins. These measurements are assumed to be realizations of a multivariate Gaussian random variable, and the maximum likelihood (ML) procedure is used to estimate its mean as $\mathbf{y}_0^b = \frac{1}{N}\sum_{j=1}^N \mathbf{y}_j^b$. This estimate is used as the known background for $t = 0$ in (4.2). Since the background typically changes over time, a method is proposed for updating the background estimate based on previous observations. Specifically, the following is proposed:

$$\mathbf{y}_{t+1}^b = \alpha(\mathbf{y}_t - \mathbf{\Phi}\Delta(\mathbf{\Phi}, \mathbf{y}_{t+1}^{ma})) + (1-\alpha)\mathbf{y}_t^b \tag{4.3}$$

$$\mathbf{y}_{t+1}^{ma} = \gamma\mathbf{y}_t + (1-\gamma)\mathbf{y}_t^{ma} \quad , \tag{4.4}$$

where $\alpha, \gamma \in (0,1)$ are learning rate parameters and $\mathbf{y}_{t+1}^{ma}$ is a moving average term. This method compensates for both gradual and sudden changes to the background. A block diagram of the proposed system is shown in Figure 2.

The above procedure assumes a fixed $\mathbf{\Phi} \in \mathbb{C}^{M \times N}$. Therefore, M compressive measurements of $\mathbf{x}_t$ are collected at time t regardless of its content. It is not hard to imagine that the number of significant components of $\mathbf{f}_t$, k_t, might vary widely with t. For example, consider a scenario in which the foreground consists of a single object at $t = t_0$, but many more at $t = t_1$. Then $k_1 > k_0$, and $M > Ck_1 \log N$ implies that $\mathbf{x}_{t_0}$ has been oversampled due to the fact that only $M > Ck_0 \log N$ measurements are necessary to obtain a good approximation of $\mathbf{f}_{t_0}$. Foregoing the ability to update the background, (Warnell et al., 2012) propose a modification to the above method for which the number of compressive measurements at each frame, M_t, can vary.

Such a scheme requires a different measurement matrix for each time instant, i.e. $\mathbf{\Phi_t} \in \mathbb{C}^{M_t \times N}$. To form $\mathbf{\Phi_t}$, one first constructs $\mathbf{\Phi} \in \mathbb{C}^{N \times N}$ via standard CS measurement matrix

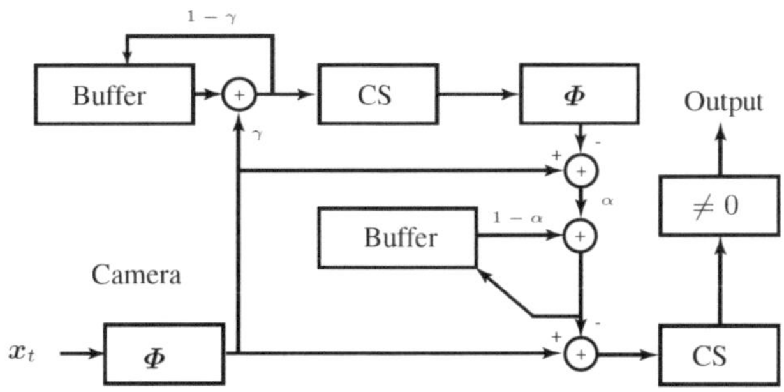

Fig. 2. Block diagram of the compressive sensing for background subtraction technique. Figure originally appears in (Cevher et al., 2008).

construction techniques. $\mathbf{\Phi_t}$ is then formed by selecting only the first M_t rows of $\mathbf{\Phi}$ and column-normalizing the result. The fixed background estimate, $\mathbf{y}^b$, is estimated from a set of measurements of the background only obtained via $\mathbf{\Phi}$. In order to use this estimate at each time instant t, $\mathbf{y}_t^b$ is formed by retaining only the first M_t components of $\mathbf{y}^b$.

In parallel to $\mathbf{\Phi}_t$, the method also requires an extra set of compressive measurements via which the quality of the foreground estimate, $\hat{\mathbf{f}}_t = \Delta(\mathbf{\Phi}_t, \mathbf{y}_t - \mathbf{y}_t^b)$, is determined. These are obtained via a *cross validation* matrix $\mathbf{\Psi} \in \mathbb{C}^{r \times N}$, which is constructed in a manner similar to $\mathbf{\Phi}$. r depends on the desired accuracy of the cross validation error estimate (given below), is negligible compared to N, and constant for all t. In order to use the measurements $\mathbf{z}_t = \mathbf{\Psi}\mathbf{x}_t$, it is necessary to perform background subtraction in this domain via an estimate of the background, $\mathbf{z}^b$, which is obtained in a manner similar to $\mathbf{y}^b$ above.

The quality of $\hat{\mathbf{f}}_\mathbf{t}$ depends on the relationship between k_t and M_t. Using a technique operationally similar to cross validation, an estimate of $\|\mathbf{f}_t - \hat{\mathbf{f}}_t\|_2$, i.e., the error between the true foreground and the reconstruction provided by Δ at time t, is provided by $\|(\mathbf{z}_t - \mathbf{z}^b) - \mathbf{\Psi}\hat{\mathbf{f}}_t\|_2$. M_{t+1} is set to be greater or less than M_t depending on the hypothesis test

$$\|(\mathbf{z}_t - \mathbf{z}^b) - \mathbf{\Psi}\hat{\mathbf{f}}_t\|_2 \lessgtr \tau_t \quad . \tag{4.5}$$

Here, τ_t is a quantity set based on the expected value of $\|\mathbf{f}_t - \hat{\mathbf{f}}_t\|_2$ assuming M_t to be large enough compared to k_t. The overall algorithm is termed *adaptive rate compressive sensing (ARCS)*, and the performance of this method compared to a non-adaptive approach is shown in Figure 3.

Both techniques assume that the tracking system can only collect compressive measurements and provide a method by which foreground images can be reconstructed. These foreground images can then be used just as in classical tracking applications. Thus, CS has provided a means by which to reduce the up-front data costs associated with the system while retaining the information necessary to track.

4.2 Kalman filtered compressive sensing

A more general problem regarding signal tracking using compressive observations is considered in (Vaswani, 2008). The signal being tracked, $\{\mathbf{x}_t\}_{t=0}^{\infty}$, is assumed to be both sparse

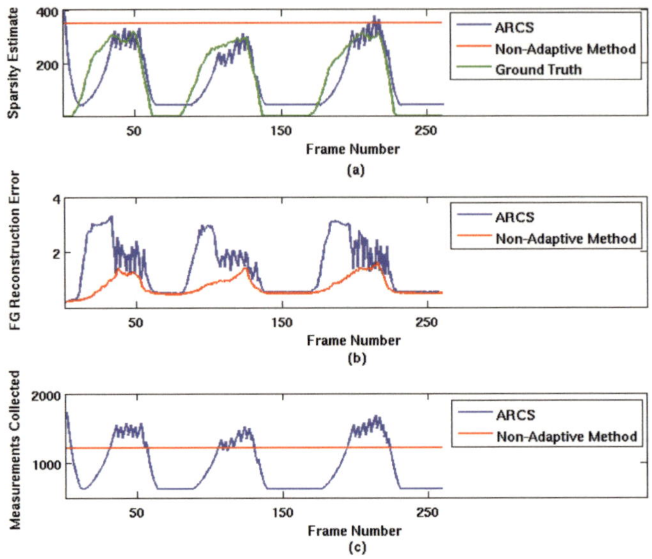

Fig. 3. Comparison between ARCS and a non-adaptive method for a dataset consisting of vehicles moving in and out of the field of view. (a) Foreground sparsity estimates for each frame, including ground truth. (b) ℓ_2 foreground reconstruction error. (c) Number of measurements required. Note the measurements savings provided by ARCS for most frames, and its ability to track the dynamic foreground sparsity. Figure originally appears in (Warnell et al., 2012).

and have a slowly-changing sparsity pattern. Given these assumptions, if the support set of $\mathbf{x}_t$, T_t, is known, the relationship between $\mathbf{x}_t$ and $\mathbf{y}_t$ can be written as:

$$\mathbf{y}_t = \mathbf{\Phi}_{T_t}(\mathbf{x})_{T_t} + \mathbf{w}_t \quad . \tag{4.6}$$

Above, $\mathbf{\Phi}$ is the CS measurement matrix, and $\mathbf{\Phi}_{T_t}$ retains only those columns of $\mathbf{\Phi}$ whose indices lie in T_t. Likewise, $(\mathbf{x}_t)_{T_t}$ contains only those components corresponding to T_t. Finally, $\mathbf{w}_t$ is assumed to be zero mean Gaussian noise. If $\mathbf{x}_t$ is assumed to also follow the state model $\mathbf{x}_t = \mathbf{x}_{t-1} + \mathbf{v}_t$ with $\mathbf{v}_t$ zero mean Gaussian noise, then the MMSE estimate of $\mathbf{x}_t$ from $\mathbf{y}_t$ can be computed using a Kalman filter instead of a CS decoder.

The above is only valid if T_t is known, which is often not the case. This is handled by using the Kalman filter output to detect changes in T_t and re-estimate it if necessary. $\tilde{\mathbf{y}}_{t,f} = \mathbf{y}_t - \mathbf{\Phi}\hat{\mathbf{x}}$, the filter error, is used to detect changes in the signal support via a likelihood ratio test given by

$$\tilde{\mathbf{y}}'_{t,f}\mathbf{\Sigma}\tilde{\mathbf{y}}_{t,f} \gtrless \tau \tag{4.7}$$

where τ is a threshold and $\mathbf{\Sigma}$ is the filtering error covariance. If the term on the left hand side exceeds the threshold, then changes to the support set are found by applying a procedure based on the Dantzig selector. Once T_t has been re-estimated, $\hat{\mathbf{x}}$ is re-evaluated using this new support set.

The above algorithm is useful in surveillance scenarios when objects under observation are stationary or slowly-moving. Under such assumptions, this method is able to perform signal tracking with a low data rate and low computational complexity.

4.3 Joint compressive video coding and analysis

(Cossalter et al., 2010) consider a collection of methods via which systems utilizing compressive imaging devices can perform visual tracking. Of particular note is a method referred to as *joint compressive video coding and analysis*, via which the tracker output is used to improve the overall effectiveness of the system. Instrumental to this method is work from theoretical CS literature which proposes a weighted decoding procedure that iteratively determines the locations and values of the (nonzero) sparse vector coefficients. Modifying this decoder, the joint coding and analysis method utilizes the tracker estimate to directly influence the weights. The result is a foreground estimate of higher quality compared to one obtained via standard CS decoding techniques.

The weighted CS decoding procedure calculates the foreground estimate via

$$\hat{\mathbf{f}} = \min_{\theta} \|\mathbf{W}\theta\|_1 \quad \text{s.t.} \quad \|\mathbf{y}^f - \mathbf{\Phi}\theta\|_2 \leq \sigma \quad , \tag{4.8}$$

where $\mathbf{y}^f = \mathbf{y} - \mathbf{y}^b$, $\mathbf{W}$ is a diagonal matrix with weights $[w(1)\ldots w(N)]$, and σ captures the expected measurement and quantization noise in $\mathbf{y}^f$. Ideally, the weights are selected according to

$$w(i) = \frac{1}{|f(i)| + \epsilon} \quad , \tag{4.9}$$

where $f(i)$ is the value of the ith coefficient in the true foreground image. Of course, these values are not known in advance, but the closer the weights are to their actual value, the more accurate $\hat{\mathbf{f}}$ becomes. The joint coding and analysis approach utilizes the tracker output in selecting appropriate values for these weights.

The actual task of tracking is accomplished using a particle filter similar to that presented in Section 2.2.2. The state vector for an object at time t is denoted by $\mathbf{z}_t = [\mathbf{c}_t\ \mathbf{s}_t\ \mathbf{u}_t]$, where $\mathbf{s}_t$ represents the size of the bounding box defined by the object appearance, $\mathbf{c}_t$ the centroid of this box, and $\mathbf{u}_t$ the object velocity in the image plane. A suitable kinematic motion model is utilized to describe the expected behavior of these quantities with respect to time, and foreground reconstructions are used to generate observations.

Assuming the foreground reconstruction $\hat{\mathbf{f}}_t$ obtained via decoding the compressive observations from time t is accurate, a reliable tracker estimate can be computed. This estimate, $\hat{\mathbf{z}}_t$, can then be used to select values for the weights $[w(1)\ldots w(N)]$ at time $t+1$. If the weights are close to their ideal value (4.9), the value of $\hat{\mathbf{f}}_{t+1}$ obtained from the weighted decoding procedure will be of higher quality than that obtained from a more generic CS decoder. (Cossalter et al., 2010) explore two methods via which the weights at time $t+1$ can be selected using $\hat{\mathbf{f}}_t$ and $\hat{\mathbf{z}}_t$. The best of these consists of three steps: *1)* thresholding the entries of $\hat{\mathbf{f}}_t$, *2)* translating the thresholded silhouettes for a single time step according to the motion model and $\hat{\mathbf{z}}_t$, and *3)* dilating the translated silhouettes using a predefined dilation element. The final step accounts for uncertainty in the change of object appearance from one frame to the next. The result is a modified foreground image, which can then be interpreted as a prediction of $\mathbf{f}_{t+1}$. This prediction is used to define the weights according to (4.9), and the weighted decoding procedure is used to obtain $\hat{\mathbf{f}}_{t+1}$.

The above method is repeated at each new time instant. For a fixed compressive measurement rate, it is shown to provide more accurate foreground reconstructions than decoders that do not take advantage of the tracker output. Accordingly, it is also the case that such a method is able to more successfully tolerate lower bit rates. These results reveal the benefit of using the high level tracker information in compressive sensing systems.

4.4 Compressive sensing for multi-view tracking

Another direct application of CS to a data-rich tracking problem is presented by (Reddy et al., 2008). Specifically, a method for using multiple sensors to perform multi-view tracking employing a coding scheme based on compressive sensing is developed. Assuming that the observed data contains no background component (this could be realized, e.g., by preprocessing using any of the background subtraction techniques previously discussed), the method uses known information regarding the sensor geometry to facilitate a common data encoding scheme based on CS. After data from each camera is received at a central processing station, it is fused via CS decoding and the resulting image or three dimensional grid can be used for tracking.

The first case considered is one where all objects of interest exist in a known ground plane. It is assumed that the geometric transformation between it and each sensor plane is known. That is, if there are C cameras, then the *homographies* $\{\mathbf{H}_j\}_{j=1}^{C}$ are known. The relationship between coordinates (u, v) in the jth image and the corresponding ground plane coordinates (x, y) is determined by $\mathbf{H}_j$ as

$$\begin{bmatrix} u \\ v \\ 1 \end{bmatrix} \sim \mathbf{H}_j \begin{bmatrix} x \\ y \\ 1 \end{bmatrix} , \qquad (4.10)$$

where the coordinates are written in accordance with their homogeneous representation. Since $\mathbf{H}_j$ can vary widely across the set of cameras due to varying viewpoint, an encoding scheme designed to achieve a common data representation is presented. First, the ground plane is sampled, yielding a discrete set of coordinates $\{(x_i, y_i)\}_{i=1}^{N}$. An occupancy vector, $\mathbf{x}$, is defined over these coordinates, where $\mathbf{x}(n) = 1$ if foreground is present at the corresponding coordinates and is 0 otherwise. For each camera's observed foreground image in the set $\{\mathbf{I}_j\}_{j=1}^{C}$, an occupancy vector $\mathbf{y'}_j$ is formed as $\mathbf{y'}_j(i) = \mathbf{I}_j(u_i, v_i)$, where (u_i, v_i) are the (rounded) image plane coordinates corresponding to (x_i, y_i) obtained via (4.10). Thus, $\mathbf{y'}_j = \mathbf{x} + \mathbf{e}_j$, where $\mathbf{e}_j$ represents any error due to the coordinate rounding and other noise. Figure 4 illustrates the physical configuration of the system.

Noting that $\mathbf{x}$ is often sparse, the camera data $\{\mathbf{y'}_j\}_{j=1}^{C}$ is encoded using compressive sensing. First, C measurement matrices $\{\mathbf{\Phi}_j\}_{j=1}^{C}$ of equal dimension are formed according to a construction that affords them the RIP of appropriate order for $\mathbf{x}$. Next, the camera

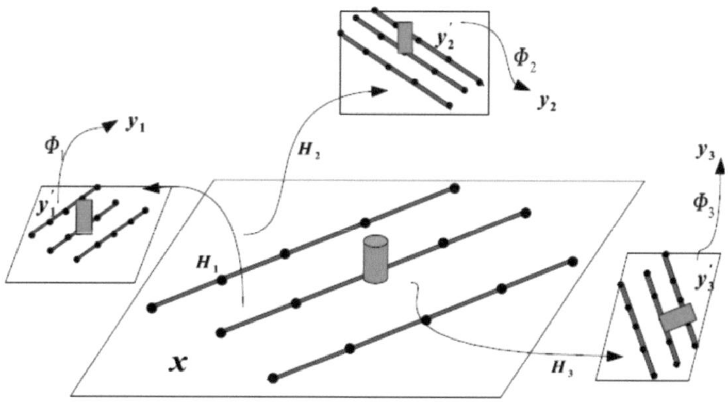

Fig. 4. Physical diagram capturing the assumed setup of the multi-view tracking scenario. Figure originally appears in (Reddy et al., 2008).

data is projected into the lower-dimensional space by computing $\mathbf{y}_j = \mathbf{\Phi}_j \mathbf{y}'_j$, $j = 1, \ldots, C$. This lower-dimensional data is transmitted to a central station, where it is ordered into the following structure:

$$\begin{bmatrix} \mathbf{y}_1 \\ \vdots \\ \mathbf{y}_C \end{bmatrix} = \begin{bmatrix} \mathbf{\Phi}_1 \\ \vdots \\ \mathbf{\Phi}_C \end{bmatrix} \mathbf{x} + \begin{bmatrix} \mathbf{e}_1 \\ \vdots \\ \mathbf{e}_C \end{bmatrix} \tag{4.11}$$

which can be written as $\mathbf{y} = \mathbf{\Phi x} + \mathbf{e}$. This is a noisy version of the standard CS problem presented in Section 3, and an estimate of $\mathbf{x}$ can be found using a relaxed version of (3.3), i.e.,

$$\hat{\mathbf{x}} = \min_{\mathbf{z} \in \mathbb{R}^N} \|\mathbf{z}\|_1 \quad \text{subject to} \quad \|\mathbf{\Phi z} - \mathbf{y}\|_2 \leq \|\mathbf{e}\|_2 \quad . \tag{4.12}$$

The estimated occupancy grid (formed, e.g., by thresholding $\hat{\mathbf{x}}$) can then be used as input to subsequent tracker components.

The above process is also extended to three dimensions, where $\mathbf{x}$ represents an occupancy grid over 3D space, and the geometric relationship in (4.10) is modified to account for the added dimension. The rest of the process is entirely similar to the two dimensional case. Of particular note is the advantage in computational complexity: it is only on the order of the dimension of $\mathbf{x}$ as opposed to the number of measurements received.

4.5 Compressive particle filtering

The final application of compressive sensing in tracking presented in this chapter is the compressive particle filtering algorithm developed by (Wang et al., 2009). As in Section 4.1, it is assumed that the system uses a sensor that is able to collect compressive measurements. The goal is to obtain tracks *without* having to perform CS decoding. That is, the method solves the sequential estimation problem using the compressive measurements directly, avoiding procedures such as (3.3). Specifically, the algorithm is a modification to the particle filter of Section 2.2.2.

First, the system is formulated in state space, where the state vector at time t is given by

$$\mathbf{s}_t = [s_t^x \; s_t^y \; \dot{s}_t^x \; \dot{s}_t^y \; \psi_t]^T \quad . \tag{4.13}$$

(s_t^x, s_t^y) and $(\dot{s}_t^x, \dot{s}_t^y)$ represent the object position and velocity in the image plane, and ψ_t is a parameter specifying the width of an appearance kernel. The appearance kernel is taken to be a Gaussian function defined over the image plane and centered at (s_t^x, s_t^y) with i.i.d. component variance proportional to ψ_t. That is, given $\mathbf{s}_t$, the jth component of the vectorized image, $\mathbf{z}_t$, is defined as

$$\mathbf{z}_t^j(\mathbf{s}_t) = C_t \exp\{-\psi_t(\begin{bmatrix} s_k^x \\ s_k^y \end{bmatrix} - \mathbf{r}^j)\} \quad , \tag{4.14}$$

where $\mathbf{r}^j$ specifies the two dimensional coordinate vector belonging to the jth component of $\mathbf{z}_t$.

The state equation is given by

$$\mathbf{s}_{t+1} = f_t(\mathbf{s}_t, \mathbf{v}_t) = \mathbf{D}\mathbf{s}_t + \mathbf{v}_t \quad , \tag{4.15}$$

where

$$D = \begin{bmatrix} 1 & 0 & 1 & 0 & 0 \\ 0 & 1 & 0 & 1 & 0 \\ 0 & 0 & 1 & 0 & 0 \\ 0 & 0 & 0 & 1 & 0 \\ 0 & 0 & 0 & 0 & 1 \end{bmatrix} \tag{4.16}$$

and $\mathbf{v}_t \sim \mathcal{N}(\mathbf{0}, \mathrm{diag}(\alpha))$ for a preselected noise variance vector α.

The observation equation specifies the mapping from the state to the observed compressive measurements $\mathbf{y}_t$. If $\mathbf{\Phi}$ is the CS measurement matrix used to sense $\mathbf{z}_t$, this is given by

$$\mathbf{y}_t = \mathbf{\Phi}\mathbf{z}_t(\mathbf{s}_t) + \mathbf{w}_t \quad , \tag{4.17}$$

where $\mathbf{w}_t$ is zero-mean Gaussian measurement noise with covariance $\mathbf{\Sigma}$.

With the above specified, the bootstrap particle filtering algorithm presented in Section 2.2.2 can be used to sequentially estimate $\mathbf{s}_t$ from the observations $\mathbf{y}_t$. Specifically, the importance weights belonging to candidate samples $\{\tilde{\mathbf{s}}_t^{(i)}\}_{i=1}^N$ can be found via

$$\tilde{w}_t^{(i)} = p(\mathbf{y}_t|\tilde{\mathbf{s}}_t^{(i)}) = \mathcal{N}(\mathbf{y}_t; \mathbf{\Phi}\mathbf{z}_t(\tilde{\mathbf{s}}_t^{(i)}), \mathbf{\Sigma}) \tag{4.18}$$

and rescaling to normalize across all i. These importance weights can be calculated at each time step without having to perform CS decoding on $\mathbf{y}$. In some sense, the filter is acting purely on compressive measurements, and hence the name "compressive particle filter."

5. Summary

This chapter presented current applications of CS in visual tracking. In the presence of large quantities of data, algorithms common to classical tracking can become cumbersome. To provide context, a review of selected classical methods was given, including background subtraction, Kalman and particle filtering, and mean shift tracking. As a means by which data reduction can be accomplished, the emerging theory of compressive sensing was presented. Compressive sensing measurements $\mathbf{y} = \mathbf{\Phi x}$ necessitate a nonlinear decoding process, which makes accomplishing high-level tracking tasks difficult. Recent research addressing this problem was presented. Compressive background subtraction was discussed as a way to incorporate compressive sensors into a tracking system and obtain foreground-only images using a reduced amount of data. Kalman filtered CS was then discussed as a computationally and data-efficient way to track slowly moving objects. As an example of using high-level tracker information in a CS system, a method that uses it to improve the foreground estimate was presented. In the realm of multi-view tracking, CS was used as part of an encoding scheme that enabled computationally feasible occupancy map fusion in the presence of a large number of cameras. Finally, a compressive particle filtering method was discussed, via which tracks can be computed directly from compressive image measurements.

The above research represents significant progress in the field of performing high-level tasks such as tracking in the presence of data reduction schemes such like CS. However, there is certainly room for improvement. Just as CS was developed by considering the integration of sensing and compression, future research in this field must jointly consider sensing and the end-goal of the system, i.e., high-level information. Sensing strategies devised in accordance with such considerations should be able to efficiently handle the massive quantities of data present in modern surveillance systems by only sensing and processing that which will yield the most relevant information.

6. References

Anderson, B. & Moore, J. (1979). *Optimal Filtering*, Dover.

Baraniuk, R. (2011). More is less: signal processing and the data deluge., *Science* 331(6018): 717–9.

Baraniuk, R. G. (2007). Compressive Sensing [Lecture Notes], *IEEE Signal Processing Magazine* 24(4): 118–121.

Broida, T. & Chellappa, R. (1986). Estimation of object motion parameters from noisy images., *IEEE Transactions on Pattern Analysis and Machine Intelligence* 8(1): 90–9.

Bruckstein, A., Donoho, D. & Elad, M. (2009). From Sparse Solutions of Systems of Equations to Sparse Modeling of Signals and Images, *SIAM Review* 51(1): 34.

Candès, E. & Wakin, M. (2008). An introduction to compressive sampling, *IEEE Signal Processing Magazine* 25(2): 21–30.

Cevher, V., Sankaranarayanan, A., Duarte, M., Reddy, D., Baraniuk, R. & Chellappa, R. (2008). Compressive sensing for background subtraction, *ECCV 2008* .

Comaniciu, D. & Meer, P. (2002). Mean shift: a robust approach toward feature space analysis, *IEEE Transactions on Pattern Analysis and Machine Intelligence* 24(5): 603–619.

Comaniciu, D., Ramesh, V. & Meer, P. (2003). Kernel-based object tracking, *IEEE Transactions on Pattern Analysis and Machine Intelligence* 25(5): 564–577.

Cossalter, M., Valenzise, G., Tagliasacchi, M. & Tubaro, S. (2010). Joint Compressive Video Coding and Analysis, *IEEE Transactions on Multimedia* 12(3): 168–183.

Doucet, A., de Freitas, N. & Gordon, N. (2001). *Sequential Monte Carlo Methods in Practice*, Springer.

Duarte, M., Davenport, M., Takhar, D., Laska, J., Kelly, K. & Baraniuk, R. (2008). Single-Pixel Imaging via Compressive Sampling, *IEEE Signal Processing Magazine* 25(2): 83–91.

Elgammal, A., Duraiswami, R., Harwood, D. & Davis, L. (2002). Background and foreground modeling using nonparametric kernel density estimation for visual surveillance, *Proceedings of the IEEE* 90(7): 1151–1163.

Isard, M. & Blake, A. (1996). Contour tracking by stochastic propagation of conditional density, *European Conference on Computer Vision* pp. 343–356.

Poor, H. V. (1994). *An Introduction to Signal Detection and Estimation, Second Edition*, Springer-Verlag.

Reddy, D., Sankaranarayanan, A., Cevher, V. & Chellappa, R. (2008). Compressed sensing for multi-view tracking and 3-D voxel reconstruction, *IEEE International Conference on Image Processing* (4): 221–224.

Romberg, J. (2008). Imaging via Compressive Sampling, *IEEE Signal Processing Magazine* 25(2): 14–20.

Sankaranarayanan, A. & Chellappa, R. (2008). Optimal Multi-View Fusion of Object Locations, *IEEE Workshop on Motion and Video Computing* pp. 1–8.

Sankaranarayanan, A., Veeraraghavan, A. & Chellappa, R. (2008). Object Detection, Tracking and Recognition for Multiple Smart Cameras, *Proceedings of the IEEE* 96(10): 1606–1624.

Stauffer, C. & Grimson, W. (1999). Adaptive background mixture models for real-time tracking, *IEEE Conference on Computer Vision and Pattern Recognition*.

Vaswani, N. (2008). Kalman filtered compressed sensing, *IEEE International Conference on Image Processing* (1): 893–896.

Wang, E., Silva, J. & Carin, L. (2009). Compressive particle filtering for target tracking, *IEEE Workshop on Statistical Signal Processing*, pp. 233–236.

Warnell, G., Reddy, D. & Chellappa, R. (2012). Adaptive Rate Compressive Sensing for Background Subtraction, *IEEE International Conference on Acoustics, Speech, and Signal Processing* .

Willett, R., Marcia, R. & Nichols, J. (2011). Compressed sensing for practical optical imaging systems: a tutorial, *Optical Engineering* 50(7).

Yilmaz, A., Javed, O. & Shah, M. (2006). Object Tracking: A Survey, *ACM Computing Surveys* 38(4).

2

A Construction Method for Automatic Human Tracking System with Mobile Agent Technology

Hiroto Kakiuchi, Kozo Tanigawa,
Takao Kawamura and Kazunori Sugahara
Melco Power Systems Co., Ltd/Graduate School of Tottori University
Japan

1. Introduction

Human tracking systems that can track a specific person is being researched and developed aggressively, since the system is available for security and a flexible service like investigation of human behaviour. For example, Terashita, Kawaguchi and others propose the method for tracking an object captured by simple active video camera (Terashita et al. 2009; Kawaguchi et al. 2008), and Yin and others propose the solution of the problem of the blurring of the active video camera (Yin et al. 2008). Tanizawa and others propose a mobile agent framework that can become the base of a human tracking system (Tanizawa et al. 2002). These are component technology, and they are available in construction of the human tracking system. On the other hand, Tanaka and others propose a human tracking system using the information from video camera and sensor (Tanaka et al. 2004), and Nakazawa and others propose a human tracking system using recognition technique which recognizes same person using multiple video cameras at the same time (Nakazawa et al. 2001). However, although these proposed systems are available as human tracking system, the systems are constructed under fixed camera position and unchanged photography range of camera. On the other hand, there are several researches to track people with active cameras. Wren and others propose a class of hybrid perceptual systems that builds a comprehensive model of activity in a large space, such as a building, by merging contextual information from a dense network of ultra-lightweight sensor nodes with video from a sparse network of high-capability sensors. They explore the task of automatically recovering the relative geometry between an active camera and a network of one-bit motion detectors. Takemura and others propose a view planning of multiple cameras for tracking multiple persons for surveillance purposes (Takemura et al. 2007). They develop a multi-start local search (MLS)-based planning method which iteratively selects fixation points of the cameras by which the expected number of tracked persons is maximized. Sankaranarayanan and others discuss the basic challenges in detection, tracking, and classification using multiview inputs (Sankaranarayanan et al. 2008). In particular, they discuss the role of the geometry induced by imaging with a camera in estimating target characteristics. Sommerlade and others propose a consistent probabilistic approach to control multiple, but diverse active cameras concertedly observing a scene (Sommerlade et al. 2010). The cameras react to objects moving about, arbitrating conflicting interests of target resolution and trajectory accuracy, and the cameras anticipate the appearance of new targets. Porikli and others propose an automatic object tracking and video summarization method for multi-camera systems with a large number of non-overlapping field-of-view cameras is explained (Porikli et al. 2003). In this framework, video sequences are stored for each object as opposed to storing a sequence for each camera.

Thus, these studies are efficient as the method to track targets. In the automatic human tracking system, tracking function must be robust even if the system loses a target person. Present image processing is not perfect because a feature extraction like ``SIFT`` (Lowe. 2004) has high accuracy but takes much processing time. The trade-off of accuracy and processing time is required for such a feature extraction algorithm. In addition, the speed a person walks is various and the person may be unable to be captured correctly in cameras. Therefore, it is necessary to re-detect a target person as tracking function even if the system loses the target. In this chapter, a construction method of human tracking system including the detection method is proposed for realistic environment using active camera like the above mentioned. And the system constructed by the method can continuously track plural people at the same time. The detection methods compensate for the above weakness of feature extraction as a function of system. The detection methods also utilize "neighbor node determination algorithm" to detect the target efficiently. The algorithm can determine neighbor camera/server location information without the location and view distance of video camera. Neighbor camera/servers are called "neighbor camera node/nodes" in this chapter. The mobile agent (Lange et al. 1999; Cabri et al. 2000; Valetto et al. 2001; Gray et al. 2002; Motomura et al. 2005; Kawamura et al. 2005) can detect the target person efficiently with knowing the neighbor camera node location information.In this chapter, the algorithm which can determine the neighbor node even if the view distance of video camera changes is also proposed.

2. System configuration

The system configuration of the automatic human tracking system is shown in Fig. 1. It is assumed that the system is installed in a given building. Before a person is granted access inside the building, the person's information is registered in the system. Through a camera an image of the persons face and body is captured. Feature information is extracted from the image by SIFT and registered into the system. Any person who is not registered or not recognized by the system is not allowed to roam inside the building. This system is composed of an agent monitoring terminal, agent management server, video recording server and feature extraction server with video camera. The agent monitoring terminal is used for registering the target person's information, retrieving and displaying the information of the initiated mobile agents, and displaying video of the target entity. The agent management server records mobile agents' tracking information history, and provides the information to the agent monitoring terminal. The video recording server records all video images and provides the images to the agent monitoring terminal via request. The feature extraction server along with the video camera analyzes the entity image and extracts the feature information from the image.

A mobile agent tracks a target entity using the feature information and the neighbor nodes information. The number of mobile agents is in direct proportion to the number of the target entities. A mobile agent is initialized at the agent monitoring terminal and launched into the feature extraction server. The mobile agent extracts the features of a captured entity and

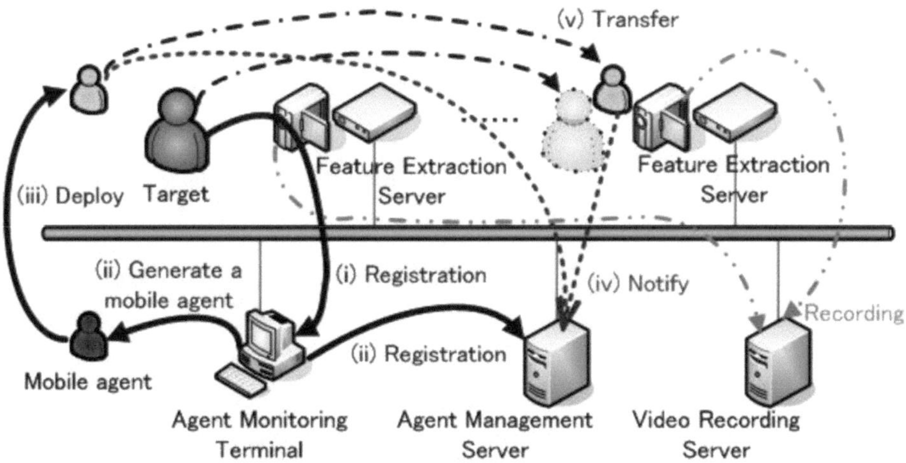

Fig. 1. System configuration and processing flow.

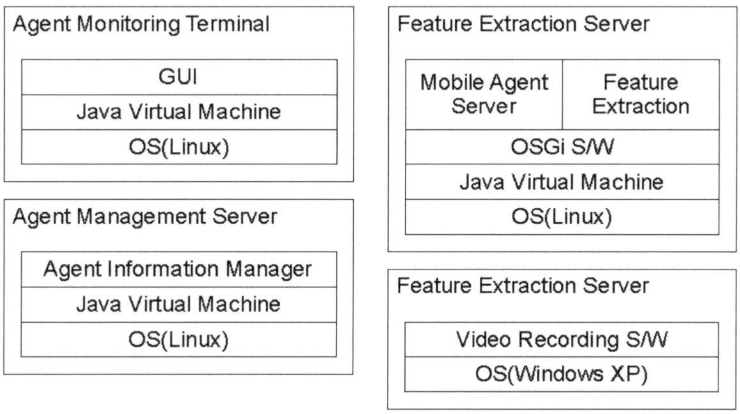

Fig. 2. System architecture.

compares it with the features already stored by the agent. If the features are equivalent, the entity is located by the mobile agent.

The processing flow of the proposed system is also shown in Fig. 1. (i) First, a system user selects an entity on the screen of the agent monitoring terminal, and extracts the feature information of the entity to be tracked. (ii) Next, the feature information is used to generate a mobile agent per target which is registered into the agent management server. (iii) Then the mobile agent is launched from the terminal to the first feature extraction server. (iv) When the mobile agent catches the target entity on the feature extraction server, the mobile agent transmits information such as the video camera number, the discovery time, and the mobile agent identifier to the agent management server. (v) Finally, the mobile agent deploys a copy of itself to the neighbor feature extraction servers and waits for the person to appear. If the mobile agent identifies the person, the mobile agent notifies the agent management server of the information, removes the original and other copy agents, and deploys the copy of itself to the neighbor feature extraction servers again. Continuous tracking is realized by repeating the above flow.

The system architecture is shown in Fig. 2. The GUI is operated only on the agent monitoring terminal. The GUI is able to register images of the entities and monitor the status of all the mobile agents. The mobile agent server is executed on the feature extraction server and allows the mobile agents to execute. The Feature extraction function is able to extract features of the captured entities, which is then utilized in the tracking of those entities as mobile agents. OSGi (Open Service Gateway Initiative Alliance) S/W acts as a mediator for the different software, allowing the components to utilize each other. The Agent information manager manages all mobile agent information and provides the information to the agent monitoring terminal. The Video recording S/W records all video, and provides the video movie to agent monitoring terminal. Each PC is equipped with an Intel Pentium IV 2.0 GHz processor and 1 GB memory. The system has an imposed condition requirement that maximum execution time of feature judgment is 1 second and maximum execution time of mobile agent transfer is 200 milliseconds.

3. Influence by change of view distance of video camera

Here is indicated a problem that a change of view distance of video camera makes change for neighbor cameras. And a solution for the problem is also indicated.

3.1 Problem of influence by change of view distance of video camera

If a mobile agent tracks a target entity, the mobile agent has to know the deployed location of the video cameras in the system. However the abilities of the neighbor cameras are also determined by their view distances. A problem caused by a difference in the view distances can occur. This problem occurs when there is a difference in expected overlap of a view or an interrupt of view.

A scenario in which a neighbor video camera's location is influenced by view distance is shown in Fig.3. The upper side figures of Fig.3 show four diagrams portraying a floor plan with four video cameras each, considering the view distances of each video camera are different and assuming that the target entity to be tracked moves from the location of video camera A to video camera D. The underside figures of Fig.3 show neighbors of each video camera with arrows. The neighbor of video camera A in object (a-1) of Fig.3 is video camera B but not C and not D as the arrows in object (a-2) show. In object (a-1) of Fig.3, video camera C and D are also not considered neighbors of video camera A, because video camera B blocks the view of video camera C and D. And the target entity can be captured at an earlier time on video camera B. But in the case of object (b-1) of Fig.3, the neighbors of video camera A are video camera B and C but not camera D as the arrows in object (b-2) of Fig. 3 show. In the case of object (c-1) of Fig.3, the neighbors of video camera A are all video cameras as the arrows in object (c-2) of Fig.3 show. Thus neighbor video camera's location indicates the difference in view distances of video cameras. The case of object (d-1) in Fig.3 is more complicated. The neighbors of video camera A in object (d-1) of Fig.3 are video camera B, C, and D as the arrows in object (d-2) of Fig.3 show. And video camera B is not considered the neighbor of video camera C. It is because video camera A exists as a neighbor between video camera B and C. When it is assumed that a target entity moves from A to D, the target entity is sure to be captured by video camera A, B, A, and C in that order.

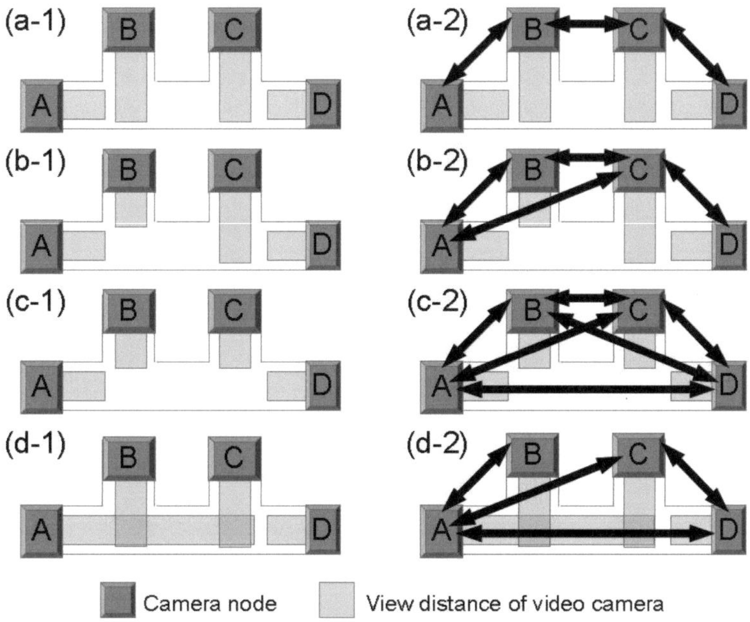

Fig. 3. Example of influence by change of view distance.

This scenario indicates that the definition of "neighbor" cannot be determined clearly because the determination of the neighbor definition is influenced by the change of view distance and it becomes more complicated as the number of video cameras increases.

3.2 Neighbor node determination algorithm to resolve the problem

Neighbor node determination algorithm can easily determine the neighbor video camera's location without regard to the influence of view distances and any modification of the information of the currently installed cameras. The modification information is set in the system to compute neighbor video cameras on the diagram, which is expressed as a graph. Nodes are used to compute neighbor video camera's information in this algorithm. The nodes are defined as camera node and non-camera node. Camera node is the location of video camera that is labeled as camera node. The nodes are defined as $A = \{a_1, a_2, ..., a_p\}$. This node is also a server with video camera. Non-camera node is defined as $V = \{v_1, v_2, ..., v_q\}$.

The conditions of a non-camera node are stated below; i) either of crossover, corner, terminal of passage, ii) the position where a video camera is installed, or iii) the end point of the view distance of a video camera. In addition, the point where the above conditions are overlapped is treated as one node. When the view distance of the video camera reaches a non-camera node, the non-camera node is defined as the neighbor of the camera node. When two non-camera nodes are next to each other on a course, those nodes are specified as neighbors. Fig.4 shows an example of these definitions applied and shows the view distances of the video cameras.

The algorithm accomplishes neighbor node determination using an adjacency matrix. Two kinds of adjacency matrix are used by the algorithm. One is an adjacency matrix X made from camera nodes' locations as rows and non-camera nodes' locations as columns. Element

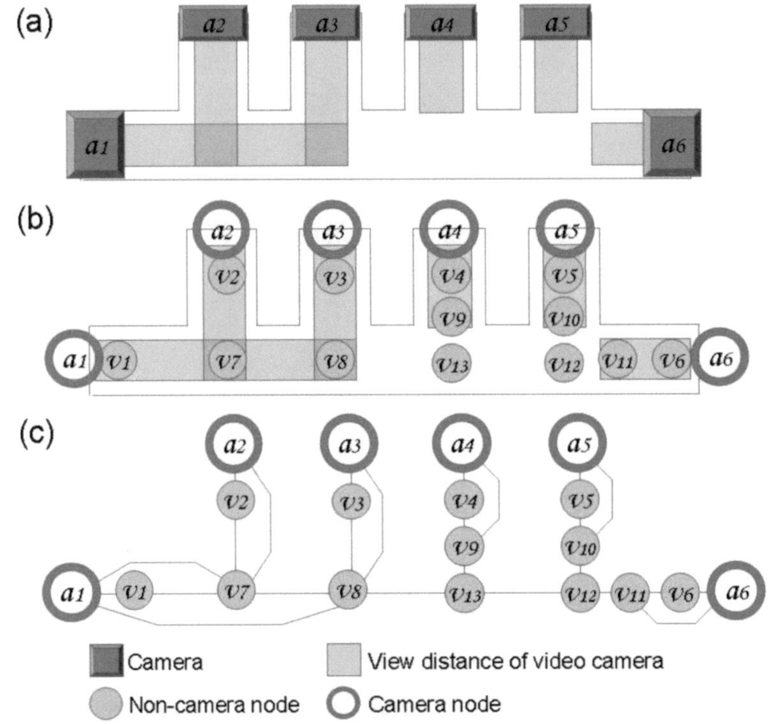

Fig. 4. Figure that sets non-camera nodes.

x_{ij} of matrix X is defined as (1). Another one is as adjacency matrix Y made from non-camera nodes' location as rows and columns. Element y_{ij} of matrix Y is defined as (2). The neighbor information for video cameras is calculated from the connection information of non-camera nodes by using adjacency matrix X and Y.

$$x_{ij} = \begin{cases} 1 & \text{There is the line which links camera node } a_i \text{ and non-camera node } v_j. \\ 0 & \text{There is no link.} \end{cases} \tag{1}$$

$$y_{ij} = \begin{cases} 1 & \text{There is the line which links two non-camera nodes, } v_i \text{ and } v_j. \\ 0 & \text{There is no link or (3) is satisfied.} \end{cases} \tag{2}$$

$$y_{ij} = y_{ji} = 1,\ \sum_{n=1}^{m} x_{ni} > 1,\ \sum_{n=1}^{m} x_{nj} > 1 \tag{3}$$

Below is the algorithm to determine neighbor nodes: i) Set camera nodes and non-camera nodes on the diagram as shown in object (b) of Fig.4. ii) Transform the diagram to a graph as shown in object (c) of Fig.4. iii) Generate an adjacency matrix X from camera node locations and non-camera node locations on the graph, and generate an adjacency matrix Y from non-camera node locations on the graph. Adjacency matrix X indicates that rows are camera nodes and columns are non-camera nodes. Adjacency matrix Y indicates that rows and columns are non-camera nodes, which results in adjacency matrix Y resolving an overlap problem of view distances between video cameras. iv) Calculate adjacency matrix X' and Y'

by excluding unnecessary non-camera nodes from adjacency matrix X and Y. v) Calculate neighbor's location matrix by multiplying adjacency matrix and transposed matrix X'^T. This neighbor's location matrix is the neighbor's node information. An unnecessary non-camera node is a non-camera node which has no camera node as a neighbor. Adjacency matrix X' and Y' are computed without unnecessary nodes, and using the procedure shown later. There are reasons why it might be better to include the unnecessary nodes in the diagram from the beginning as we have done. Since the risk of committing an error will be higher as the diagram becomes larger, we include the unnecessary nodes from the beginning and remove them at the end. Finally, matrix E which indicates the neighbor nodes is derived as (4).

$$E = X'Y'X'^T \begin{cases} \geq 1 & a_i \text{ is neighbour node to } a_j. \\ = 0 & a_i \text{ is not neighbour node to } a_j. \end{cases} \tag{4}$$

4. Human tracking method

Human tracking method consists of Follower method and Detection method. Follower method is used for tracking a moving target. Detection method is used for detecting a target when an agent has lost the target. In the tracking method, an agent has three statuses as "Catching", "Not catching" and "Lost". At first, an agent is assumed that it stays on a certain camera node. If the feature parameter the agent keeps is similar to the feature parameter extracted on the node, agent's status is indicated as "Catching". If the parameter the agent keeps is not similar to the feature parameter extracted on the node, agent's status is indicated as "Not catching". If the agent keeps "Not catching" status on a certain time, the agent decides that it lost a target, and agent's status is indicated as "Lost".

4.1 Follower method

In Follower method, an agent deploys its copies to neighbor nodes when agent's status becomes "Catching". When one of the copies has "Catching" status, all agents except that copy are removed from the system. And that copy becomes original agent. After that, the agent deploys its copies to neighbor nodes again. The follower method realizes tracking by repeating those routine.

4.2 Detection method

The detection method in this chapter is used to re-detect a target when the automatic tracking system loses the target. This method improves the tracking function, because an individual can not be accurately identified in the current image processing. As such the reliability of the system is further improved, because it enhances the continuous tracking function and re-detection of the target even if a target is lost for a long period of time. In this chapter, if a target is not captured within a certain period of time, the mobile agent then concludes that the target is lost. On such case the system can also conclude that the target is lost.

We are proposing two types of detection method: (a) "Ripple detection method" and (b) "Stationary net detection method". These methods are shown in Fig. 5.

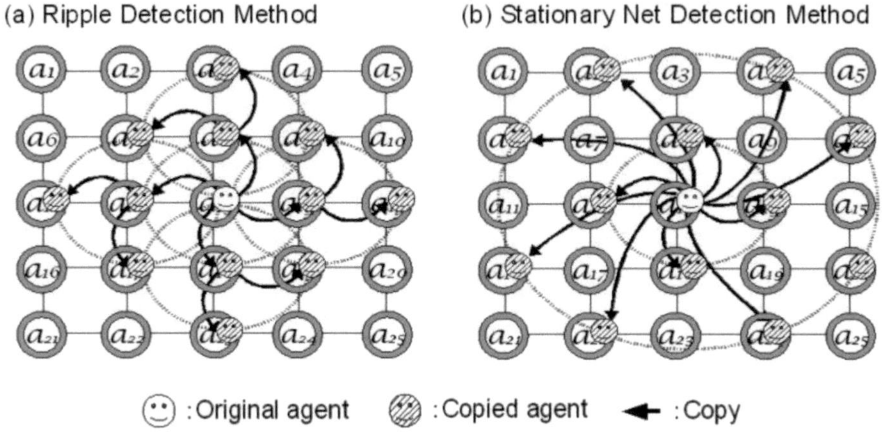

Fig. 5. Figure that sets non-camera nodes.

Ripple detection method widens a search like a ripple from where an agent lost a target to give top priority to re-detect. This method has a feature that the discovery time becomes shorter and usual tracking can resume more quickly, if the target exists near where the agent lost. In addition, this method deletes other agents immediately after discovering the target, and suppresses the waste of the resource. The Ripple detection method is developed and is experimented in search propriety. In the Ripple detection method, the neighbor camera nodes are shown as (5).

$$E1 = E = X'Y'X'^{T} \tag{5}$$

When a mobile agent lost a target, copy agents are deployed to the next nodes of (5) expressed by (6), and search is started. E^2 shows next neighbor camera nodes, because the elements of E^2 larger than 1 can be reached if the elements are larger than 1. Therefore, except neighbor node information E of camera nodes, automatic human tracking system uses a minimum resource by deploying copy agents.

$$E2 = E^2 - E1 = E^2 - E \tag{6}$$

Similarly, it becomes like (7) and (8) to calculate the next camera node further.

$$E3 = E^3 - (E2 + E1) = E^3 - E^2 \tag{7}$$

$$E4 = E^4 - (E3 + E2 + E1) = E^4 - E^3 \tag{8}$$

As mentioned above, the equation (9) is derived when deploying agents efficiently to the n next camera nodes. n is larger than 2 and is incremented one by one when this equation is used for detection.

$$En = E^n - \sum_{m=1}^{n-1} Em = E^n - E^{n-1} \tag{9}$$

Stationary net detection method widens a search like setting a stationary net with the Neighbor node determination algorithm from where an agent lost a target to give top priority to re-detect. This method uses equation (10) in the algorithm.

$$E = X'(Y')^{n-1} X'^{T} \begin{cases} \geq 1 & a_i \text{ is neighbour node to } a_j. \\ = 0 & a_i \text{ is not neighbour node to } a_j. \end{cases} \tag{10}$$

In this equation, adjacency matrix E indicates the node that can reach via n non-camera nodes and n is always set to $n \geq 2$. In this method, the coefficient n is set to $n = 4$ because camera nodes are set with a certain interval. The interval between cameras in the real system may be close, but in that case, number of non-camera nodes between the cameras decreases. Therefore it is enough interval to re-detect a target if n consists of $n \geq 4$. This method has a feature that agents are deployed to neighbor camera nodes via n next non-camera nodes and catch a target like a stationary net. In addition, this method also deletes other agents immediately after discovering the target, and suppresses the waste of the resource. The Stationary net detection method is developed and is experimented in search property. In the Stationary net detection method, the neighbor camera nodes are shown as (11).

$$E1 = E = X'Y'X' \tag{11}$$

When a mobile agent lost a target, copy agents are deployed to the next nodes of (11) expressed by (12), and search is started. $X'Y'^2X'^T$ shows neighbor camera nodes via two non-camera nodes, because the elements of $X'Y'^2X'^T$ larger than 1 can be reached if the elements are larger than 1. If copy agents are deployed at each camera nodes via non-camera nodes more than two, detection range of target widens. And, excepting neighbor node information E of camera nodes, automatic human tracking system uses a minimum resource by deploying copy agents.

$$E2 = X'Y'^2 X'^T - E. \tag{12}$$

Similarly, it becomes like (13) and (14) to calculate the next camera node of more wide range.

$$E3 = X'Y'^3 X'^T - (E2 + E1) \tag{13}$$

$$E4 = X'Y'^4 X'^T - (E3 + E2 + E1) \tag{14}$$

As mentioned above, the equation (15) is derived when deploying agents efficiently to the next camera nodes via n non-camera nodes. n is larger than 2 and is incremented one by one when this equation is used for detection.

$$En = X'Y'^n X'^T - \sum_{m=1}^{n-1} Em = X'Y'^n X'^T - X'Y'^{n-1} X'^T \tag{15}$$

5. Experimentation

Here are two types of experiment. One is an experiment by simulator, and the other one is an experiment by real environment. In the experiment by simulator, follower method and detection methods are experimented, and the effectiveness is verified. In the experiment by real environment, the tracking method is verified for whether the plural targets can be tracked continuously.

5.1 Experiment by simulator

Examination environment for the Ripple detection method and the Stationary net detection method is shown in Fig. 6 and Fig. 7. There are twelve camera nodes in the environment of floor map 1, and there are fourteen camera nodes in the environment of floor map 2. Here, the following conditions are set in order to examine the effectiveness of these detection methods. i) Camera nodes are arranged on latticed floor, $56m \times 56m$. ii) View distance of camera is set to $10m$ in one direction. iii) Identification of a target in the image processing does not fail when re-detecting. iv) Walking speed of the target is constant. v) Only one target is searched. vi) The target moves only forward without going back. In the case of the floor map 1, the target moves following the order of a_1, a_2, a_3, a_4, a_5, a_6, a_7, a_8, a_9, a_{10}, a_{11}, a_{12} and a_1. In the case of the floor map 2, the target moves following the order of a_1, a_2, a_4, a_5, a_7, a_9, a_{10}, a_{11} and a_1. In the examination, the time that an agent concludes a failure of tracking is same as search cycle time. The search cycle time is defined as the time concluded that an agent can not discover a target. The search cycle time is prepared using 3 patterns 12 seconds, 9 seconds and 6 seconds. Walking speed of the target is prepared using 3 patterns $1.5m/s$, $2m/s$ and $3m/s$. And search of target is prepared that an agent loses a target at a_7 and the agent starts a search in the situation that the target has already moved to a_8. Furthermore, Stationary net detection method is examined by 3 patterns $n = 2$, $n = 3$ and $n = 4$, because of confirming effectiveness by number of non-camera nodes. On each floor map, using 12 patterns of such combination by each walking speed, discovery time and the number of agents are measured. Generally, the walking speed of a person is around $2.5m/s$, and the two types of walking speed, $2m/s$ and $3m/s$, used by the target which was examined are almost equivalent to the walking speed of general person. And walking speed, $1.5m/s$, is very slow from the walking speed of general person.

The results of the measurement on the floor map 1 are shown in Table 1, Table 2 and Table 3. The results of the measurement on the floor map 2 are shown in Table 4, Table 5 and Table 6. They are a mean value of 5 measurements.

The result of the Ripple detection method shows that the discovery time becomes shorter and usual tracking can resume more quickly, if the target exists near where the agent lost. But, if the walking speed of a target is faster, the agent will become difficult to discover the target.

The result of the Stationary net detection method shows that the agent can discover a target if coefficient n has larger value, even if the walking speed of a target is faster. And it is not enough interval to re-detect a target if n consists of $n \leq 3$ and it is not enough time to re-detect the target if the search cycle time is shorter.

From the result of measurement on the floor map 1, if the Stationary net detection method uses coefficient $n = 4$, there is not the difference of efficiency between the Ripple detection method and the Stationary net detection method. However, from the result of measurement

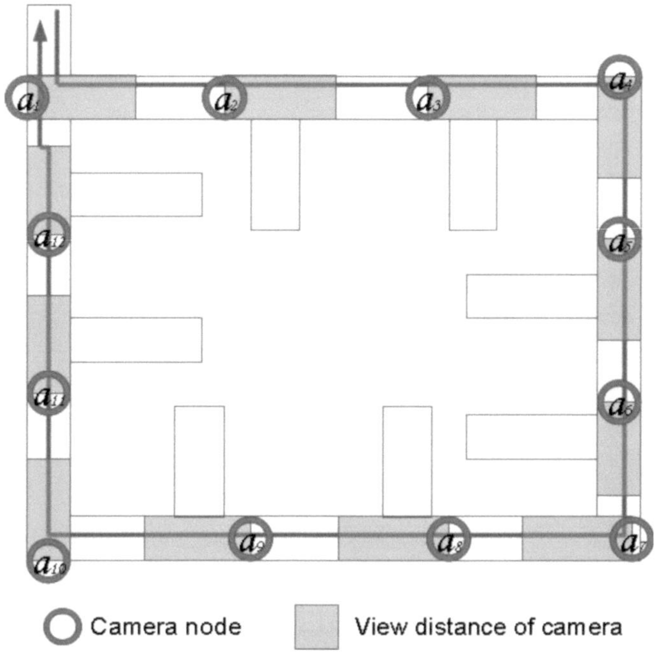

Fig. 6. Floor map 1 for experiment of detection methods.

on the floor map 2, if a floor map is complicated, the discovery time of the Stationary net detection method becomes shorter than the discovery time of the Ripple detection method and the number of agents of the Stationary net detection method becomes less than the number of agents of the Ripple detection method.

On the whole, the result of both methods shows that a number of agents decreases by searching a target near search cycle but the agents can not search the target if the search cycle time is longer than the waking speed. In addition based on the results, when the walking speed is faster, the discovery time is shortened or equal and the number of agents decreases or is equal.

Walking Speed (1.5*m/s*)		Ripple	Stationary Net (n=2)	Stationary Net (n=3)	Stationary Net (n=4)
Search Cycle(12*s*)	Number of Agents	6	12	12	6
	Discovery Time (*s*)	20.6	-	-	20.5
Search Cycle(9*s*)	Number of Agents	6	12	6	6
	Discovery Time (*s*)	20.5	-	20.5	20.5
Search Cycle(6*s*)	Number of Agents	7	6	6	7
	Discovery Time (*s*)	20.5	20.5	20.5	20.5

Table 1. Detection time on floor map 1 by walking speed 1.5*m/s*.

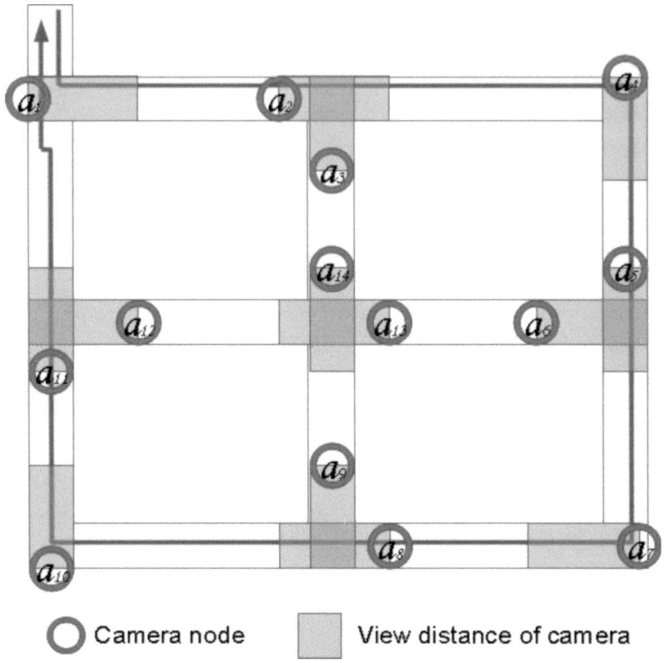

Fig. 7. Floor map 2 for experiment of detection methods.

Walking Speed (2*m/s*)		Ripple	Stationary Net (n=2)	Stationary Net (n=3)	Stationary Net (n=4)
Search Cycle(12*s*)	Number of Agents	6	12	12	6
	Discovery Time (*s*)	15.5	-	-	15.5
Search Cycle(9*s*)	Number of Agents	6	12	12	6
	Discovery Time (*s*)	15.5	-	-	15.4
Search Cycle(6*s*)	Number of Agents	7	12	6	7
	Discovery Time (*s*)	16.5	-	15.5	15.7

Table 2. Detection time on floor map 1 by walking speed 2*m/s*.

Walking Speed (3*m/s*)		Ripple	Stationary Net (n=2)	Stationary Net (n=3)	Stationary Net (n=4)
Search Cycle(12*s*)	Number of Agents	12	12	12	12
	Discovery Time (*s*)	-	-	-	-
Search Cycle (9*s*)	Number of Agents	5.9	12	12	6
	Discovery Time (*s*)	11.7	-	-	11.5
Search Cycle(6*s*)	Number of Agents	6	12	12	6
	Discovery Time (*s*)	11.7	-	-	11.6

Table 3. Detection time on floor map 1 by walking speed 3*m/s*.

Walking Speed (1.5*m/s*)		Ripple	Stationary Net (n=2)	Stationary Net (n=3)	Stationary Net (n=4)
Search Cycle(12*s*)	Number of Agents	14	14	10	12.2
	Discovery Time (*s*)	49.5	-	31.8	32.6
Search Cycle(9*s*)	Number of Agents	13.8	10	10	13
	Discovery Time (*s*)	33.7	32.3	32.3	33
Search Cycle(6*s*)	Number of Agents	13.9	10	13.2	14
	Discovery Time (*s*)	32.2	32	32.4	33

Table 4. Detection time on floor map 2 by walking speed 1.5*m/s*.

Walking Speed (2m/s)		Ripple	Stationary Net (n=2)	Stationary Net (n=3)	Stationary Net (n=4)
Search Cycle(12*s*)	Number of Agents	14	14	10	10
	Discovery Time (*s*)	-	-	31.1	25.3
Search Cycle(9*s*)	Number of Agents	14	14	10	13
	Discovery Time (*s*)	35.9	-	25.6	25.2
Search Cycle(6*s*)	Number of Agents	13.8	10	13	14
	Discovery Time (*s*)	24.8	25.3	24.8	25.8

Table 5. Detection time on floor map 2 by walking speed 2*m/s*.

Walking Speed (3*m/s*)		Ripple	Stationary Net (n=2)	Stationary Net (n=3)	Stationary Net (n=4)
Search Cycle(12*s*)	Number of Agents	14	14	14	9.8
	Discovery Time (*s*)	-	-	-	18
Search Cycle(9*s*)	Number of Agents	14	14	14	10
	Discovery Time (*s*)	-	-	-	18.2
Search Cycle(6*s*)	Number of Agents	14	14	10.4	12.4
	Discovery Time (*s*)	25.9	-	18.2	19

Table 6. Detection time on floor map 2 by walking speed 3*m/s*

5.2 Experiment by real environment

Upon verification of real system, it aimed to confirm whether targets can be tracked continuously by tracking method. Therefore, in order to reduce influence by image processing performance, the image processing adopts simple processing by color vision. In this experiment, there is a miniature environment of 2*m* by 2*m* shown in Fig. 8 and Fig. 9. Here are three targets and those targets have each moving routes, red, blue, and green, shown in Fig. 8. The environment consists of seven servers with USB camera. The toys are used as targets instead of people tracked. This toy is a train toy with a sensor that recognizes a black line. And the train runs on along the line. The black line is used as a route a target walks and is drawn by hand. The toy is covered with a color paper to keep a certain accuracy of image processing as shown in Fig. 9. The moving speed of target is 6.8*m/second*. This environment has simulated a floor of 60*m* by 60*m* on the scale of 1/30; therefore the

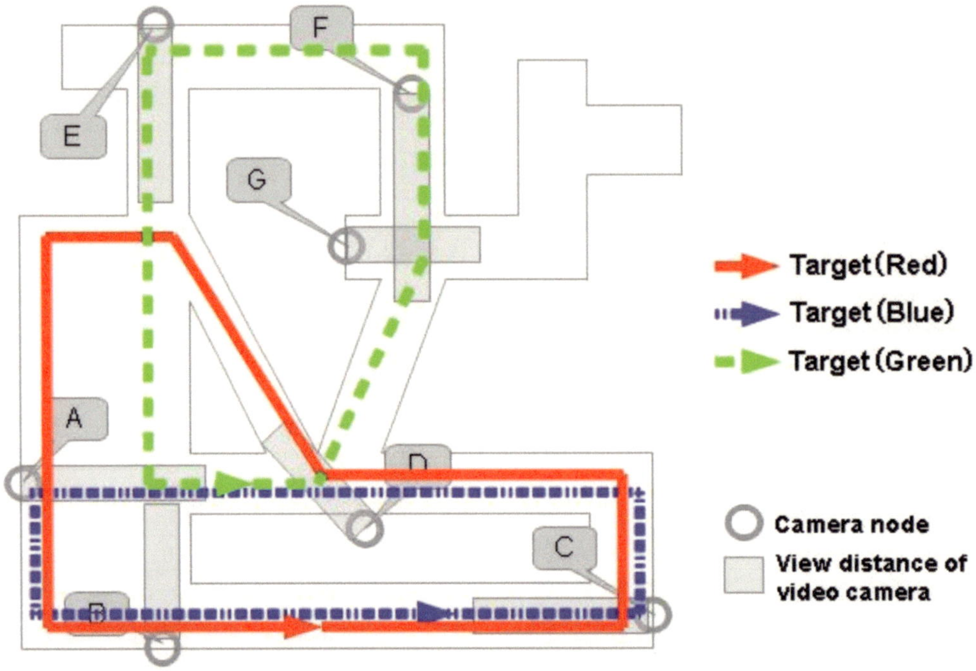

Fig. 8. Moving route of targets on experiment environment.

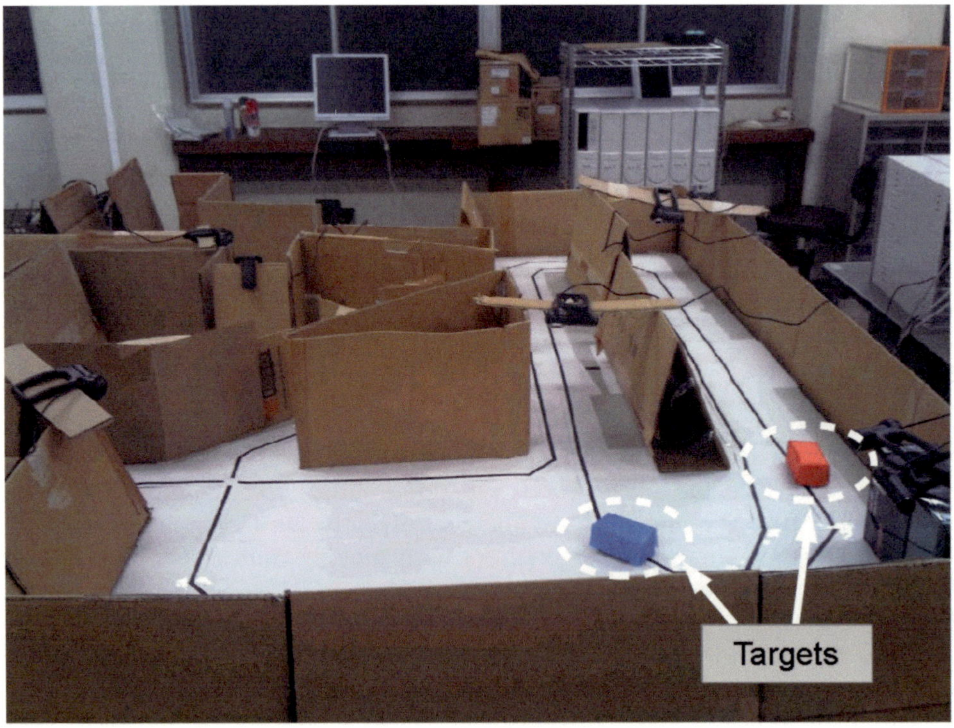

Fig. 9. Real experiment environment.

moving speed of the target is equivalent to 2.0*m/second*. Consider the moving route and the moving speed of the target, the search cycle is set to 5 seconds.

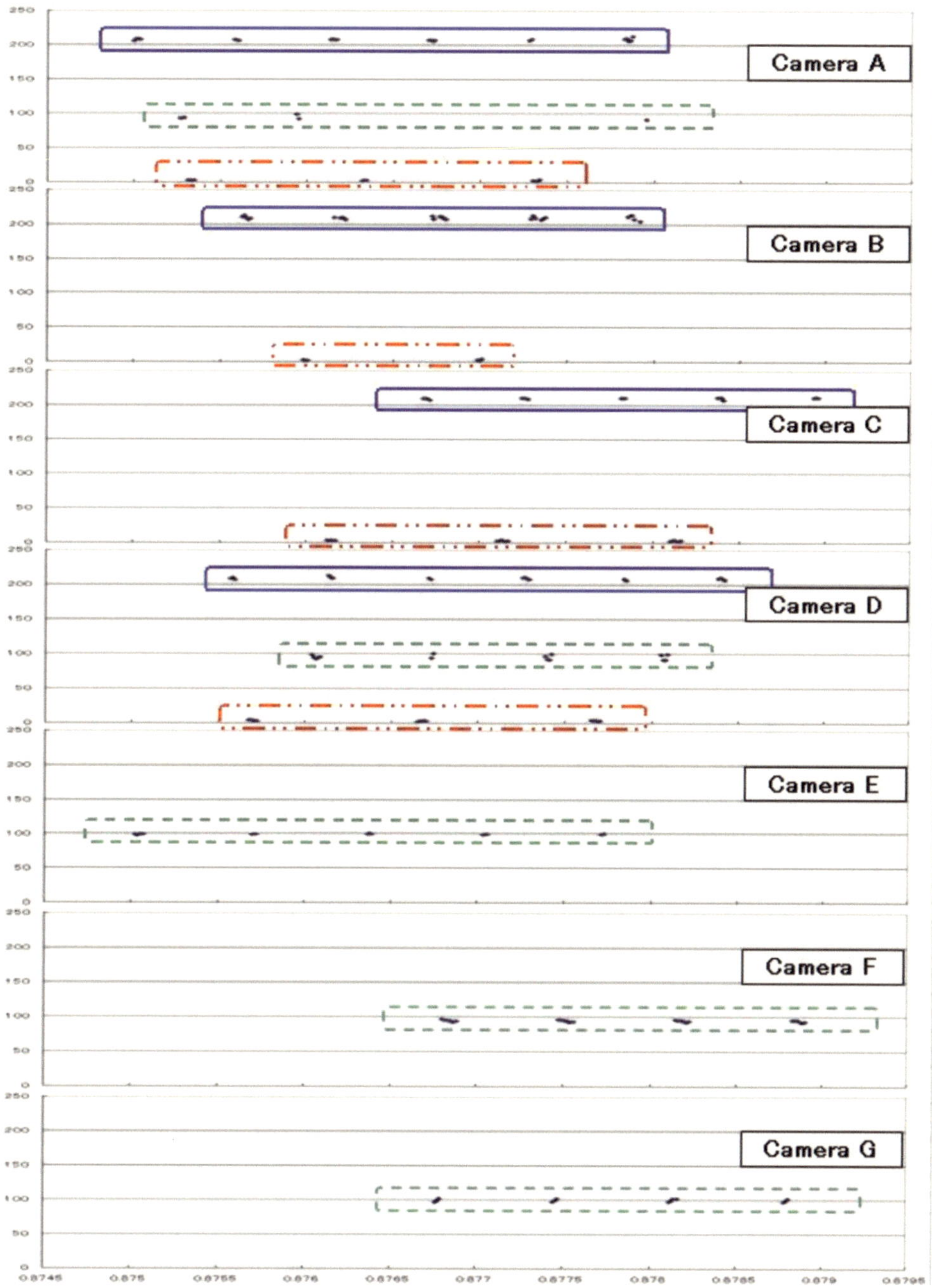

Fig. 10. Detection of target by camera on experiment environment.

Fig. 10 shows the result in the experiment. The graph of Fig. 10 is arranged in order from camera A to camera G. Horizontal axis is time and the vertical axis is the value of the extracted H-HVS color. A solid line rectangle encloses the part where a red target was discovered, the rectangle of the short dashed line encloses the part where a blue target was discovered, and a dotted line rectangle encloses the part where a green target was discovered. The plot becomes a constant pattern if target is captured correctly, because the movement of the target is periodic. However, The illuminance was actually different according to the place that the camera installed, the color was judged the black by the shadow, and the target might not be able to be caught. Therefore, the number of agents did not increase and decrease by a constant pattern. But, the Neighbor node determination algorithm was able to calculate neighbor camera nodes. However, when the target is captured by video camera, the neighbor nodes are recomputed by the algorithm, then it was confirmed that an agent might not be deployed appropriately for a few dozens milliseconds. About this result, it is necessary to improve the computation time. In graphs of Fig. 10, the plot shows the time the target captured. It is confirmed that a target is lost temporarily from the camera capturing the target. But it is confirmed that the human tracking keeps tracking targets continuously by capturing the target by other cameras.

6. Conclusion

A construction method of automatic human tracking system with mobile agent technology is proposed using neighbor node determination algorithm. The construction method consists of the neighbor node determination algorithm and tracking methods. The neighbor node determination algorithm can compute neighbor nodes. This algorithm can be efficient to compute neighbor node and can make the system robust even if view distance of camera is changed. The tracking methods consist of follower method and detection method. The follower method can identify feature of a target locally. The detection method can search a lost target but a search cycle has to be within *walking speed* × *distance between cameras*. The detection method can be efficient to detect a target if the search cycle is near the walking speed. A mobile agent can keep tracking a target by using these detection methods if the agent lost the target. In addition, from the experiment results, the Stationary net detection method can detect a target faster than the Ripple detection method. And the Stationary net detection method can use smaller number of agents than the Ripple detection method. Because the Ripple detection method searches a target by widening a search gradually but the Stationary net detection method can widen a search efficiently by the Neighbor node determination algorithm.

The effectiveness of proposed tracking method was experimented using simulator and real environment. In the experiment using simulator, the tracking methods are experimented by the walking speed of a target. In the detection methods, consideration is added about the propriety of the parameter n which gives the number of non-camera nodes. Aimed to confirming behavior of the automatic human tracking system, the system in a real environment uses the simple image processing which can identify the color information of a target except the influence by the accuracy of image processing. And the follower method and the detection method are confirmed to be effective by a toy instead of a targeted person and to be able to construct the automatic human tracking system.

We will research more efficient detection to improve the automatic human tracking system. In addition, the accuracy of image processing has to be improved more to track a target more accurately. We are considering to improve our tracking system by combining effective studies and to improve image processing program by using PCA-SIFT (Ke et al. 2004) or SURF (Bay et al. 2008) algorithm.

7. Acknowledgment

The authors would like to thank Tadaaki Shimizu, Yusuke Hamada, Naoki Ishibashi, Shinya Iwasaki, Hirotoshi Okumura, Masato Hamamura, and Shingo Iiyama in Tottori University.

8. References

Terashita, K.; Ukita, N. & Kidode, M. (2009). Efficiency improvement of probabilistic-topological calibration of widely distributed active cameras, *IPSJ SIG Technical Report*, vol. 2009–CVIM–166, pp. 241–248

Kawaguchi, Y.; Shimada, A.; Arita, D. & Taniguchi, R. (2008). Object trajectory acquisition with an active camera for wide area scene surveillance, *IPSJ SIG Technical Report*, vol. 2008–CVIM–163, pp. 1306–1311

Yin, H. & Hussain, I. (2008). Independent component analysis and nongaussianity for blind image deconvolution and deblurring, *Integrated Computer-Aided Engineering*, vol. 15, No. 3, pp. 219–228

Tanizawa, Y.; Satoh, I. & Anzai, Y. (2002). A User Tracking Mobile Agent Framework "FollowingSpace", *Information Processing Society of Japan*, Vol. 43, No. 12, pp. 3775-3784

Tanaka, T.; Ogawa, T.; Numata, S.; Itao, T.; Tsukamoto, S. & Nishio, S. (2004). Design and Implementation of a Human Tracking System Using Mobile Agents in Camera and Sensor Networks, *IPSJ Workshop of Groupware and Network services 2004*, pp. 15-20

Nakazawa, A.; Hiura, S.; Kato, H. & Inokuchi, S. (2001). Tracking Multiple Persons Using Distributed Vision Systems, *Information Processing Society of Japan*, Vol. 42, No. 11, pp. 2699-2710

C. R. Wren, U. M. Erdem, and A. J. Azarbayejani, Automatic pan-tilt-zoom calibration in the presence of hybrid sensor networks, *Proceedings of the Third ACM International Workshop on Video Surveillance & Sensor Networks (VSSN'05)*, pp. 113–120, Nov. 2005.

N. Takemura & J. Miura, View planning of multiple active cameras for wide area surveillance, *Proc. IEEE International Conference on Robotics and Automation (ICRA'07)*, pp. 3173–3179, Apr. 2007.

Aswin C. Sankaranarayanan, Ashok Veeraraghavan & Rama Chellappa, Object Detection, Tracking and Recognition for Multiple Smart Cameras, *Proceedings of the IEEE*, vol. 96(10), pp. 1606-1624, Oct 2008

Sommerlade, E. & Reid, I. , Probabilistic Surveillance with Multiple Active Cameras, *Robotics and Automation (ICRA), 2010 IEEE International Conference on* , vol., no., pp.440-445, 3-7 May 2010

Alexandros Iosifidis & Spyridon G. Mouroutsos, A Hybrid Static/Active Video Surveillance System, *Antonios Gasteratos International Journal of Optomechatronics*, 1559-9620, Volume 5, Issue 1, Pages 80 – 95, January 2011

F. Porikli and A. Divakaran, Multi-Camera Calibration, Object Tracking and Query Generation, *Proc. International Conference on Multimedia and Expo (ICME'03)*, pp. 653–656, July 2003.

Lange, D. B. & Oshima, M. (1999). Seven good reasons for mobile agents, *Communications of the ACM*, vol. 42, no. 3, pp. 88–89

Gray, R. S.; Cybenko, G.; Kotz, D.; Peterson, R. A. & Rus, D. D. (2002). D 'agents: Applications and performance of a mobile-agent system, *Software: Practice and Experience*, vol. 32, no. 6, pp. 543–573

Motomura, S.; Kawamura, T. & Sugahara, K. (2005). Maglog: A mobile agent framework for distributed models, *Proceedings of the IASTED International Conference on Parallel and Distributed Computing and Systems*, pp. 414–420

Kawamura, T.; Motomura, S. & Sugahara, K. (2005). Implementation of a logic-based multi agent framework on java environment, *Proceedings of IEEE International Conference on Integration of Knowledge Intensive Multi-Agent Systems*, pp. 486–491

Cabri, G.; Leonardi, L. & Zambonelli, F. (2000). Mobile-agent coordination models for internet applications," *Computer*, vol. 33, no. 2, pp. 82–89, February 2000

Valetto, G.; Kaiser, G. & Kc, G. S. (2001). A mobile agent approach to process-based dynamic adaptation of complex software systems, *Lecture Notes in Computer Science*, vol. 2077, pp. 102–116

Lowe, D. G. (2004). Distinctive image features from scale-invariant keypoints, *International Journal of Computer Vision*, vol. 60, no. 2, pp. 91–110

Ke, Y. & Sukthankar, R. (2004). Pca-sift: A more distinctive representation for local image descriptors, *Computer Vision and Pattern Recognition (CVPR)*, vol. 2, pp. 506–513

Bay, H.; Ess, A.; Tuytelaars, T. & Gool, L. V. (2008). Speeded-up robust features (surf), *Computer Vision and Image Understanding (CVIU)*, vol. 110, no. 3, pp. 346–359

Open Service Gateway Initiative Alliance, *OSGi Alliance Specifications OSGi Service Platform Release 1*, last access May 2011. [Online]. Available: http://www.osgi.org/Specifications/HomePage

3

Appearance-Based Retrieval for Tracked Objects in Surveillance Videos

Thi-Lan Le[1], Monique Thonnat[2] and Alain Boucher[3]
[1]*MICA Center, HUST - CNRS/UMI 2954 - Grenoble INP, Hanoi,*
[2]*PULSAR, INRIA Sophia Antipolis,*
[3]*IFI, MSI Team; IRD, UMI 209 UMMISCO; Vietnam National University,*
[1,3]*Vietnam*
[2]*France*

1. Introduction

Video surveillance is a rapidly growing industry. Driven by low-hardware costs, heightened security fears and increased capabilities, video surveillance equipment is being deployed more widely and with greater storage than ever. This provides a huge amount of video data. Associating to these video data, retrieval facilities become very useful for many purposes and many kinds of staff. Recently, several approaches have been dedicated to retrieval facilities for surveillance data (Le, Thonnat et al. 2009) (Zhang, Chen et al. 2009). Figure 1 shows how indexing and retrieval facility can be integrated in a surveillance system. Videos coming from cameras will be interpreted by the video analysis module. There are two modes for using the analysed results: (1) the corresponding alarms are sent to members of the security staff to inform them about the situation; (2) the analysed results are stored in order to be used in the future. In this chapter, we focus on analysing current achievements in surveillance video indexing and retrieval. Video analysis (Senior 2009) is beyond the scope of this chapter.

Video analysis module provides two main result types of result: objects and events. Thus, surveillance video indexing and retrieval approaches can divided into two categories: surveillance video indexing and retrieval at the object level (Calderara, Cucchiara et al. 2006; Ma and Cohen 2007; Le, Thonnat et al. 2009) and at the event level (Zhang, Chen et al. 2009; Velipasalar, Brown et al. 2010). As events of interest may vary significantly among different applications and users, this chapter focuses on presenting the work done for surveillance video indexing and retrieval at the object level.

The remaining of the chapter is organized as follows: In Section 2, we give a brief overview of surveillance object retrieval. Section 3 aims at analysing in detail appearance-based surveillance object retrieval. We first give some definitions and point out the existing challenges. Then, we describe the solutions proposed for two important tasks: object signature building and object matching in order to overcome these challenges. Section 4 presents current achievements and discusses about open problems in this domain.

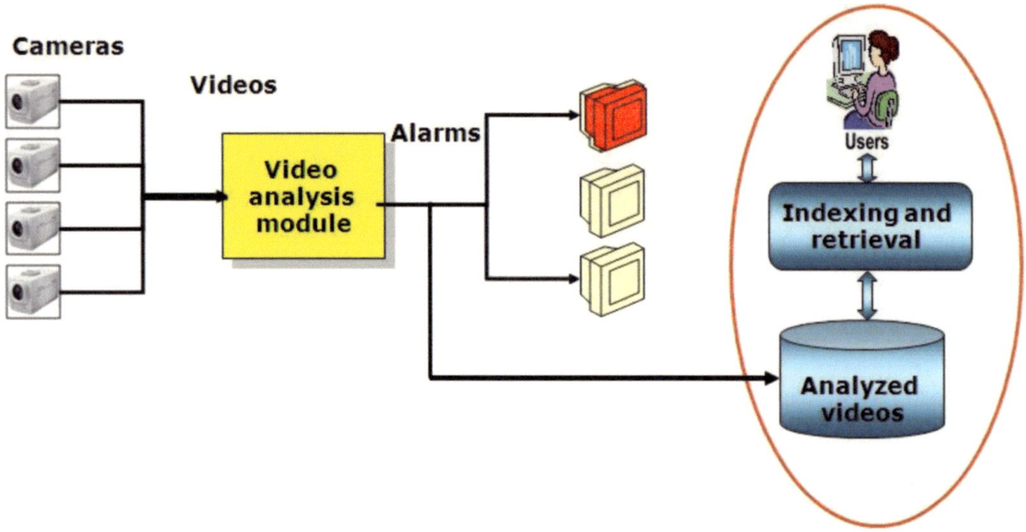

Fig. 1. Indexing and retrieval facility in a surveillance system. Videos coming from cameras will be interpreted by the video analysis module. There are two modes for using the analysed results: (1) the corresponding alarms are sent to security staffs to inform them about the situation; (2) the analysed results are stored in order to be used in the future.

2. Object retrieval for surveillance videos

This section aims to give an overview of existing approaches for object retrieval in surveillance videos.

2.1 Architecture

In the same way as video analysis systems which have two main architectures, i.e. centralized and decentralized architecture (Senior 2009), object video retrieval for surveillance systems has also two main modes: late fusion and early fusion modes. In the late fusion mode (cf. Fig. 2), the object detection and tracking are performed on the video stream of each camera. Then, the object matching compares the query and the detected objects for each camera. The matching results are fused to form the retrieval results. In the early fusion mode (cf. Fig. 3), the data fusion is done in the object detection and tracking module. We can see that the object retrieval method in this early fusion mode has more opportunities to obtain a good result because if an object is not totally observed by a camera, it may be well captured by other cameras. Most of the state of the art work belongs to the early fusion mode. However, the fusion strategy is not explicitly discussed except in the work of Calderara et al. (Calderara, Cucchiara et al. 2006).

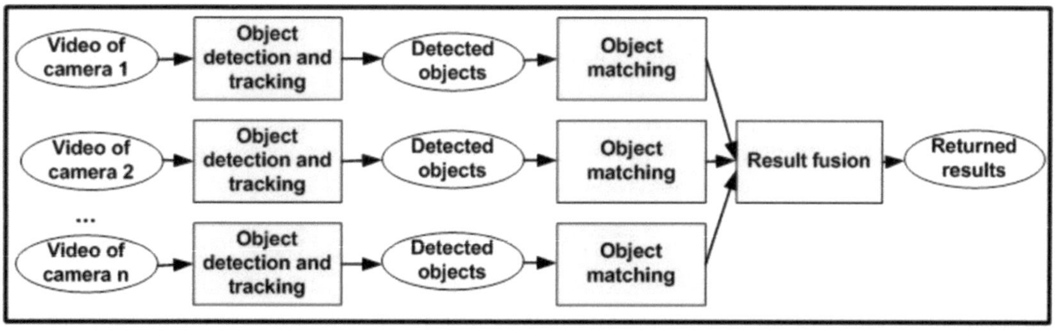

Fig. 2. Late fusion object retrieval approach: the object detection and tracking is performed on video stream of each camera. Then, the object matching compares the query and the detected objects of each camera. The matching result is then fused to form the retrieval results.

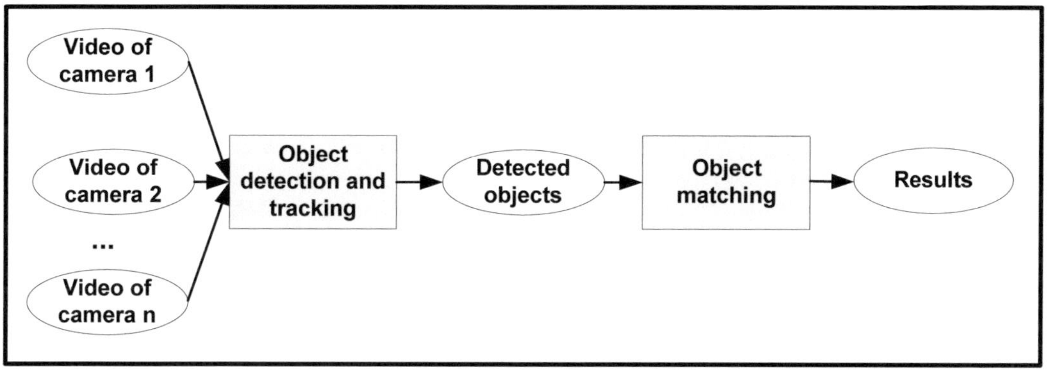

Fig. 3. Early fusion object retrieval approach.

2.2 Object feature extraction and representation

Since objects in video surveillance are physical objects (e.g. people, vehicles) that are present in the scene at a certain time, in general, they are detected and tracked in a large number of frames. Objects in videos possess two main characteristics named spatial and temporal characteristics. Spatial characteristics of an object may be its positions in frames (in 2D coordinates) and positions in scene (in 3D coordinates), its spatial relationships with other objects and its appearance. Temporal characteristics of an object contain its movement and its temporal relationships with other objects. Therefore, an object may be represented by one sole or several characteristics. However, among these characteristics, object movement and object appearance are the two most important characteristics and are widely used in the literature.

Concerning the object representation based on object movement, in the literature, a number of different approaches have been proposed for object movement representation and matching (Broilo, Piotto et al. 2010). Certain approaches directly use detected object positions across frames that are represented in trajectory form (Zheng, Feng et al. 2005). As object trajectory may be very complex, other authors try to segment an object trajectory into several sub-trajectories (Buchin, Driemel et al. 2010) with the purpose that each subtrajectory represents a relatively stable pattern of object movement. Other work attempts to move to higher levels of object trajectory representation, named symbolic level and semantic level. At symbolic level, (Chen, Ozsu et al. 2004; Hsieh, Yu et al. 2006; Le, Boucher et al. 2007) aim to convert object trajectory into a character sequence. The advantage is that they promote the applying of successful and famous methods in text retrieval such as the Edit Distance for object trajectory matching. The approaches dedicated to object trajectory representation at the semantic level try to learn the semantic meaning such as turn left, low speed from object movement (Hu, Xie et al. 2007). As results, the output is close to the human manner of thinking. However, they strongly depend on applications.

Object representation based on its appearance has attracted a lot of research interest. Appearance-based object retrieval methods for surveillance video are distinguished each other by two criteria. The first criterion is the appearance feature extracted on the image/frame where the object is detected and the second one is the way to create object signature from all features extracted over the object's life time and to match objects based on their signatures. In the next section, we describe in detail the object signature building and object matching methods. In this section, we only present the object appearance feature.

There is a great variety of object features used for surveillance object representation. In fact, all features that are proposed for image retrieval can be applied for surveillance object representation. Appearance object features can be divided into two categories: global and local. Global features are color histogram, dominant color, covariance matrix, just to name a few. Besides global features, local features such as interest points and SIFT descriptor can be extracted from the object's region.

In (Yuk, Wong et al. 2007), the authors have proposed to use MPEG-7 descriptors such as dominant colors, edge histograms for surveillance retrieval. In the context of one research project conducted by IBM research center[1], the researchers have evaluated a large number of color features for surveillance application that are standard color histograms, weighted color histograms, variable bin size color histograms and color correlograms. Results show color correlogram to have the best performance. Ma et Cohen (Ma and Cohen 2007) suggest to use the covariance matrix as object feature. According to the authors, the covariance matrix is appealing because it fuses different types of features and has small dimensionality. The small dimensionality of the model is well suited for its use in surveillance videos because it takes very little storage space. In our research (Le, Boucher et al. 2010), we have evaluated the performance of 4 descriptors which are dominant color, edge histogram, covariance matrix (CM) and SIFT descriptor for surveillance object representation and matching. The obtained results show that if the objects are detected while the background and context objects are not present in the object region, the used descriptors allow retrieving objects with relatively good results. For other cases, the covariance matrix is more effective than the other descriptors. According to our experiments, it is interesting to see that when the covariance matrix represents information of all pixels in a blob, the points of interest use only few pixels. The dominant color and the edge histogram use the approximate information of pixel color and edge. A pair of descriptors (covariance matrix and dominant color) or (covariance matrix and edge histogram) or (covariance matrix and SIFT descriptors) may be chosen as default descriptors for object representation.

[1] https://researcher.ibm.com/researcher/view_project.php?id=1393

3. Appearance-based object retrieval in surveillance videos

In this section, we firstly give some definitions and point out the existing challenges for appearance-based object retrieval in surveillance videos. Then, we describe the solutions proposed for two important tasks: object signature building and object matching in order to overcome these challenges.

3.1 Definitions

Definition 1: An **object blob** is a region determined by a minimal bounding box in a frame where the object is detected.

The minimal bounding box is calculated by the object detection module in video analysis and an object has one sole minimal bounding box. Fig. 4 gives some examples of detected objects and their corresponding blobs.

Fig. 4. Detected objects and their blobs (Bak, Corvee et al. 2010).

Definition 2: Object representation

In surveillance applications, one object is in general detected and tracked in a number of frames. In other words, a set of object blobs is defined for an object. Therefore, an object can be represented as:

$$O = \{B_i\}, i \in 1, N \tag{1}$$

where O is object, B_i is the ith object blob, N is the total number of blobs of object O.

It is worth noting that object blobs can be non-consecutive since an object may not be detected in certain frames and the value of N varies depending on the object life time in the scene. Fig. 5 gives an example of an object that is represented by its blobs. As we can notice, with poor object detection, several object blobs do not cover well the object appearance.

Fig. 5. An object is represented by its blobs.

3.2 Challenges in appearance-based object retrieval for surveillance videos

This section aims at pointing out existing challenges in appearance-based object retrieval for surveillance videos. As object indexing and retrieval take the output of video analysis as its input (cf. Fig. 1), the quality of the video analysis has a huge influence on object indexing and retrieval. Current achievements on surveillance video analysis show that video analysis is far from perfect since it is hampered by issues in low resolution, pose and lighting variations and object occlusion. In this section, we point out the challenges in appearance-based object retrieval by analyzing the effect of two modules of video analysis on the object indexing and retrieval quality: the object detection and the object tracking modules.

The object detection module is the module that allows to determine the object blobs. An object detection module is good if all blobs of a detected object (1) cover totally this object and (2) do not contain other objects. However, these constraints are not always met. Object retrieval has to address three difficult cases as shown in Fig. 6. In the first case, the object is not present at all in the blob (Fig. 6a). With the second case, the object is partially present in the blob (Fig. 6b) while with the third case, the blob of the detected object covers totally this object, however, it contains also other objects (Fig. 6c and Fig. 6d).

Concerning the object tracking quality, two metrics that are widely used for evaluating the performance of object tracking in the video surveillance community are *object ID persistence* and *object ID confusion* (Nghiem, Bremond et al. 2007). The *object ID persistence* metric helps to evaluate the ID persistence. It computes over the time how many tracked objects (output of the object tracking module) are associated to one ground-truth object. On the contrary, the *object ID confusion* metric computes the number of objects per detected object (having the same ID). A good object tracking algorithm obtains a small value for these two metrics (minimum is 1).

Fig. 6. Examples of object detection quality (a) The object is not present in the blob; (b) The object is partially present in the blob; (c) and (d) The object is totally present in the blob.

However, the obtained results in several video surveillance benchmarks show that current achievement on object tracking is still limited (object ID persistence and object ID confusion metrics are generally much greater than 1). Fig. 7 shows an example of the object ID persistence problem: two tracked objects created for one sole ground-truth object, therefore object ID persistence is equal to 2. Fig. 8 illustrates an example of object ID confusion: three ground-truth objects IDs associated to one sole detected object (object ID confusion = 3).

Fig. 7. An example of the object ID persistence problem: two tracked objects created for one sole ground-truth object (object ID persistence = 2).

Based on the above-mentioned analysis, the main challenge in surveillance object indexing and retrieval is the poor quality of object detection and tracking. An object indexing and retrieval algorithm is robust if it can work with different quality of the object detection and tracking.

With the object representation as defined in Eq. 1, we believe that object indexing and retrieval methods can address the poor quality of object detection and tracking problem if they have an effective object signature building and a robust object matching.

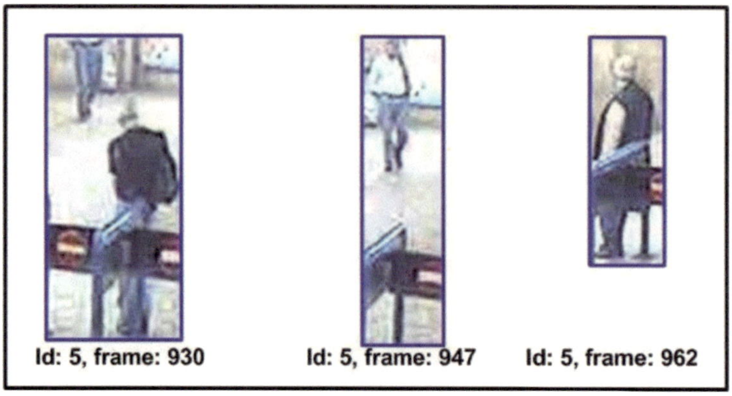

Fig. 8. An example of object ID confusion: three ground-truth object IDs associated to one sole detected object (object ID confusion = 3).

3.3 Object signature building

Object signature building is a process that aims at calculating one or a set of descriptors, named object signature, from a set of object blobs.

The calculated signature should (1) be able to represent all object appearance aspects, (2) be distinctive and (3) be as compact as possible. Among these characteristics, the two first characteristics ensure the robustness of the retrieval part. The third characteristic relates to the effectiveness of the indexing part. If the signature is compact, it does not require much storage.

Object signature building methods for surveillance video are divided into two approaches. The first object signature building approach is based on the following observation: Surveillance objects are generally detected and tracked in a large number of frames. Consequently, an object is represented by a set of blobs. Due to errors in object detection, using all these blobs for object indexing and retrieval is irrelevant. Moreover, it is redundant because of the similar content between blobs (two consecutive blobs of an object are closely similar). Based on this observation, methods belonging to the first approach try to select the most relevant and representative blobs from a set of blobs and then to compute object features on these blobs. This process is defined by Eq. 2. This approach is composed of two steps. The first step, called representative blob detection, chooses from the object blobs the most relevant and representative ones that represent significantly the object appearance while the second step computes the object features mentioned in Section 2.2 from the calculated representative blobs.

$$\left\langle \{B_i\}, i \in 1,N \right\rangle \overset{(1)}{\rightarrow} \left\langle \{Br_j\}, j \in 1,M \right\rangle \overset{(2)}{\rightarrow} \left\langle \{F_j\}, j \in 1,M \right\rangle \quad \text{with } N \gg M \tag{2}$$

where:

- $\left\langle \{B_i\}, i \in 1,N \right\rangle$: set of original blobs for the object O determined by using object detection output.

- $\langle\{Br_j\}, j \in 1, M\rangle$: set of representative blobs detected for the object O.
- $\langle\{F_j\}, j \in 1, M\rangle$: set of features extracted on the representative blobs. The extracted feature can be color histogram, dominant color, etc.

Instead of calculating only the representative blobs, several authors compute a set of pairs: the representative blob and its associating weight while the weight associated with a representative blob shows the importance of this blob. With this, the first approach is defined as follows:

$$\langle\{B_i\}, i \in 1, N\rangle \overset{(1)}{\rightarrow} \langle\{Br_j, w_j\}, j \in 1, M\rangle \overset{(2)}{\rightarrow} \langle\{F_j, w_j\}, j \in 1, M\rangle$$
$$\text{with } N \gg M \text{ and } \sum_{j=1}^{M} w_j = 1 \quad (3)$$

Fig. 9 shows an example of the first object signature building approach. From a large number of blobs (905 blobs), the object signature building method selects only 4 representative blobs. Their associated weights are 0.142, 0.005, 0.016 and 0.835.

Fig. 9. An example of representative blob detection: 4 representative blobs are extracted from 905 blobs.

The methods presented in (Ma and Cohen 2007) and in (Le, Thonnat et al. 2009) are the most significant ones of the first object signature building approach. These methods are distinguished each from the other by the way to define the representative blobs.

The representative blob detection method proposed by Ma et Cohen (Ma and Cohen 2007) is based on the agglomerative hierarchical clustering and the covariance matrix extracted from the object blobs. This method is composed of the three following steps:

Step 1. Do agglomerative clustering on the original set of object blobs based on the covariance matrix.
Step 2. Remove clusters having a small number of elements.
Step 3. Select representative blobs.

The first step aims at forming clusters of similar blobs. The similarity of two blobs is defined by using the covariance matrix. The covariance matrix is built over a feature vector f, for each pixel, that is: $f(x,y)=[x, y, R(x, y), G(x, y), B(x, y), \nabla R^T(x, y), \nabla G^T(x, y), \nabla B^T(x, y)]$ where R, G, B are the colorspace axes and x, y are the coordinates of the pixel contributing to the color and the gradient information. The covariance matrix is computed for each detected blob as follows:

$$C = \sum_{x,y} (f - \bar{f})(f - \bar{f})^T \tag{4}$$

The covariance matrices for blobs of different sizes have the same size. In fact, the covariance matrix is a N×N matrix while N is the dimension of the feature vector f.

The distance between two blobs is calculated as:

$$d(C_i, C_j) = \sqrt{\sum_{k=1}^{d} \ln^2 \lambda_k(C_i, C_j)} \tag{5}$$

For the agglomerative clustering, the distance $d(A,B)$ between two clusters A and B is computed by average linkage as:

$$d(A,B) = \frac{1}{|A|.|B|} \sum_{A_i \in A} \sum_{B_j \in B} d(A_i, B_j) \tag{6}$$

where $d(A_i, B_j)$ is defined in Eq. 5.

The objective of the second step is to detect and remove outliers that are clusters containing a small number of elements. The final step determines one representative blob for each cluster. For a cluster B, the representative blob B_l is defined as:

$$l = \arg\min_{j=1,\dots,|B|, j \neq i} \sum_{i=1,\dots,|B|} d(B_i, B_j) \tag{7}$$

where $d(B_i, B_j)$ is the blob distance defined in Eq. 5.

Fig.10 gives an example result of Ma and Cohen method (Ma and Cohen 2007): (a) original sequence of blobs; (b) clustering results having valid cluster and invalid cluster; (c) representative frame for the second cluster in (b); (d) representative frame for the third cluster in (b). We can see that this method can dominate errors of the object detection if they occur in a small number of frames. However, if the detection error occurs in a large number of frames, the cluster containing the blobs of these frames will be defined as valid cluster by this method (the validity of clusters is decided by their sizes).

Our work presented in (Le, Thonnat et al. 2009) is an improvement of Ma and Cohen work (Ma and Cohen 2007), based on two remarks. The first remark is that the drawback of Ma and Cohen's method is that it cannot work well with imperfect object detection since it processes all object blobs including relevant and irrelevant ones. We can resolve this drawback by removing all irrelevant blobs before doing the agglomerative clustering. The second remark is that one blob of an object is relevant if it contains this object or objects belonging to the same class of this object. For example, one blob of a detected person is relevant if it represents somehow the person class. With these analyses, we add two

(a)

(b)

(c) (d)

Fig. 10. Example result of Ma and Cohen method (Ma and Cohen 2007): (a) original sequence of blobs; (b) clustering results having valid clusters and invalid clusters; (c) representative frame for the second cluster in (b); (d) representative frame for the third cluster in (b).

preliminary steps in Ma and Cohen's work. These steps will be performed before the first step of Ma and Cohen's work.

Step 0. Classify blobs of all objects into relevant (with the object of interest) and irrelevant blobs (without object of interest) by a two-class SVM classifier with radial basis function (RBF) kernel using edge histograms (Won, Park et al. 2002).

Step 1. Remove irrelevant blobs from the set of blobs for each object.

It is worth noting that the appearance of tracked objects may vary but their blobs usually have some common visual characteristics (e.g. human shape characteristics for the blobs of different tracked persons). As we can see, the two added steps allow to remove irrelevant blobs before agglomerative clustering. Therefore, this object signature building method is robust while working with poor quality object detection.

The second object signature building approach does not perform explicitly the representative blob detection. It attempts to sum up all object appearances into one sole signature. This approach is defined as follows:

$$\langle \{B_i\}, i \in 1, N \rangle \rightarrow \langle \tilde{F} \rangle \quad (8)$$

The work presented in (Calderara, Cucchiara et al. 2006) belongs to the second object signature building approach. In this work, the authors have proposed three notations that are person's appearance (PA), single camera appearance trace (or SCAT in short) and multicamera appearance trace (or MCAT in short). SCAT of the person P on camera C_i is composed of all the past person's appearance (PA) of P at instant time t:

$$SCAT_i^P = \left\{ PA_i^P(t) \mid t = 1, \ldots N_i^P \right\} \quad (9)$$

where t represents the samples in time in which the person P was visible from the camera C_i and N_i^P is the total number of frames in which he was visible and detected.

MCAT for a person P is composed of all the $SCAT_i^P$ for any camera C_i in which, at the current moment, the person P has been detected at least for one frame. We can see that SCAT is equivalent to MCAT if the surveillance system has only a camera and SCAT is equivalent to $\langle \{B_i\}, i \in 1, N \rangle$ in our definition.

The object signature building based on mixture of Gaussians is performed as follows:

Step 1. Using the first PA in the MCAT, the ten principal modes of the color histogram are extracted;

Step 2. The Gaussians are initialized with a mean μ equal to the color corresponding to the mode and a fixed variance σ^2; weights are equally distributed for each Gaussian;

Step 3. successive PA belonging to the MCAT are processed to extract again the ten main modes that are used to update the mixture; then, for each mode:

- (a) its value is checked against the mean of each Gaussian and if for none of them the difference is within 2.5σ of the distribution, the mode generates a new Gaussian (using the same process reported above) replacing the existing Gaussian with the lowest weight;
- (b) the Mahalanobis distance is computed for every Gaussian satisfying the above-reported check, and the mode is assigned to the nearest Gaussian; the mean and the variance of the selected Gaussian are updated with the following adaptive equations:

$$\begin{aligned} \mu_t &= (1-\alpha)\mu_{t-1} + \alpha X_t \\ \sigma_t^2 &= (1-\alpha)\sigma_{t-1}^2 + \alpha (X_t - \mu_t)^T (X_t - \mu_t) \end{aligned} \quad (10)$$

where X_t is the vector with the values corresponding to the mode and α is the fixed learning factor; the weights are also updated by increasing that of the selected Gaussian and decreasing those of the other Gaussians consequently.

At the end of this process, ten Gaussians and the corresponding weights for each MCAT are available and are used as object signature.

3.4 Object matching

Object matching is the process that computes the similarity/dissimilarity between two objects based on their signatures calculated by above-mentioned approaches. In information retrieval in general and in surveillance object retrieval in particular, with a given query, the system will (1) compute the similarity between this query and all elements in the database and (2) return the retrieved results which are a list of elements sorted by their similarity with the query. The number of returned results will be decided for each application.

Corresponding to the two approaches for object signature building, there are two approaches for the object matching. Object matching for the first object signature building approach is expressed in Eq. 11. In this equation, object O_q and O_p are represented by $\{(F_i^q, w_i^q) \mid i \in 1, M^q\}$ and $\{(F_j^p, w_j^p) \mid j \in 1, M^p\}$ respectively. The object matching methods allow to define a similarity/dissimilarity between two sets of blobs. These sets may have different sizes. It is worth noting that we can always compute the similarity/dissimilarity of a pair of blobs based on visual features such as color histogram, covariance matrix.

$$\begin{aligned}&\left\langle \{(Br_i^q, w_i^q) \mid i \in 1, M^q\}, \{(Br_j^p, w_j^p) \mid j \in 1, M^p\} \right\rangle \rightarrow Dis, Dis \in \Re \text{ or} \\ &\left\langle \{(F_i^q, w_i^q) \mid i \in 1, M^q\}, \{(F_j^p, w_j^p) \mid j \in 1, M^p\} \right\rangle \rightarrow Dis, Dis \in \Re\end{aligned} \tag{11}$$

In (Ma and Cohen 2007), the authors define a similarity measure between two objects O_q and O_p using the Hausdorff distance (Eq. 12). The Hausdorff distance is the maximum distance of a set to the nearest point in the other set.

$$\begin{aligned}Dis &= Hausdorff\left(\{(F_i^q, w_i^q) \mid i \in 1, M^q\}, \{(F_j^p, w_j^p) \mid j \in 1, M^p\}\right) \\ &= \max_{i \in M^q} \min_{j \in M^p} d(F_i^q, F_j^p)\end{aligned} \tag{12}$$

where $d(F_i^q, F_j^p)$ is the distance between two blobs by using the covariance matrix.

The above object matching allows to take into consideration multiple appearance aspects of the object being tracked. However, the Hausdorff distance is not relevant when working with object tracking algorithms having a high value of object ID confusion because this distance is extremely sensitive to outliers. If two sets of points A and B are similar, all the points are perfectly superimposed except only one single point in A which is far from any point in B, then the Hausdorff distance determined by this point.

In (Le, Thonnat et al. 2009), we propose a new object matching based on the EMD (Earth Mover's Distance) (Rubner, Tomasi et al. 1998). This method is widely applied with success in image and scripted video retrieval.

$$Dis = EMD\left(\{(F_i^q, w_i^q) \mid i \in 1, M^q\}, \{(F_j^p, w_j^p) \mid j \in 1, M^p\}\right) \tag{13}$$

Computing the EMD is based on a solution to the old transportation problem. This is a bipartite network flow problem which can be formalized as the following linear programming problem: Let I be a set of suppliers, J a set of consumers, and c_{ij} the cost to ship a unit of supply from $i \in I$ to $j \in J$. We want to find a set of flows f_{ij} that minimizes the overall cost:

$$\sum_{i \in I} \sum_{j \in J} f_{ijc_{ij}} \tag{14}$$

subject to the following constraints:

$$\begin{aligned} & f_{ij} \geq 0, i \in I, j \in J \\ & \sum_{i \in I} f_{ij} = y_j, j \in J \\ & \sum_{j \in J} f_{ij} \leq x_i, i \in J \\ & \sum_{j \in J} y_j \leq \sum_{i \in I} x_i \end{aligned} \tag{15}$$

where x_i is the total supply of supplier i and y_j is the total capacity of consumer j. Once the transportation problem is solved, and we have found the optimal flow $F^* = \{f^*_{ij}\}$, the EMD is defined as:

$$EMD = \frac{\sum_{i \in I} \sum_{j \in J} f^*_{ij} c_{ij}}{\sum_{j \in J} y_j} \tag{16}$$

When applied to surveillance object matching, the cost c_{ij} becomes the distance of two blobs and the total supply x_j and y_j are the blob weights. c_{ij} can be various descriptor distance between two blobs such as color histogram distance, covariance matrix.

In comparison with the matching method based on the Hausdorff distance (Ma and Cohen 2007), our matching method based on the EMD distance possesses two precious characteristics. Firstly, it considers the participation of each blob in computing the distance based on its similarity with other blobs and its weight. Thanks to the representative blob detection method, blob weight expresses the important degree of this blob in object representation. The proposed matching method ensures a minor participation of irrelevant blobs produced by errors in object tracking because these blobs are relatively different from other blobs and have a small weight. Therefore, the matching method is robust when working with object tracking algorithms having a high value of *Object Id Confusion*. Secondly, the proposed object matching allows partial matching.

We analyze here an example of these object matching methods: We want to compute the similarity/dissimilarity between object O_q with 4 representative blobs and object O_p with 5 representative blobs (Fig. 12). The *Object Id Confusion* values of the object tracking module for the first object and the second object are 2 and 1 respectively.

In order to carry out object matching, firstly, we need to compute the distance of each pair of blobs. Tab. 1 shows the distance of each pair of blobs computed on covariance matrix distance (cf. Eq. 5) while Fig. 12 presents the result of object matching methods. Hausdorff-based object matching is determined by the distance between blob 1 of object O_q and blob 5 of object O_p (dot line) while EMD-based object matching search for an optimal solution with the participation of each blob. This example shows how the EMD-based object matching method overcomes the poor object tracking challenge.

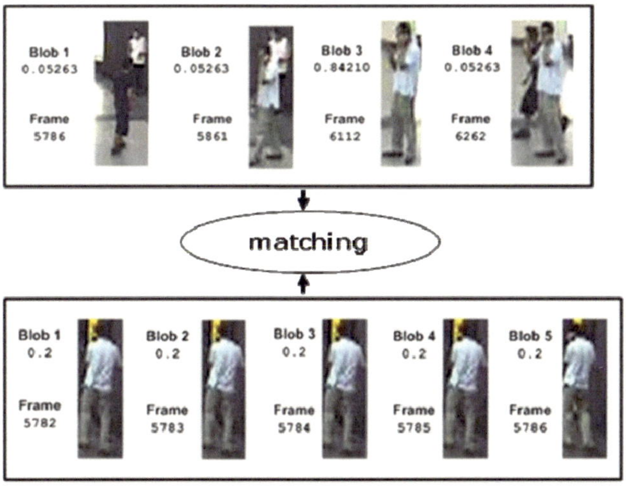

Fig. 11. Matching between object O_q with 4 representative blobs and object O_p with 5 representative blobs.

	Object O_p					
Object O_q	***Blob***	***Br_1^p***	***Br_2^p***	***Br_3^p***	***Br_4^p***	***Br_5^p***
	Br_1^q	3.873	3.873	3.873	3.873	3.361
	Br_2^q	2.733	2.733	2.733	2.733	2.161
	Br_3^q	2.142	2.142	2.142	2.142	1.879
	Br_4^q	2.193	2.193	2.193	2.193	2.048

Table 1. Distance of each pair of blobs of O_q and O_p based on covariance matrix distance

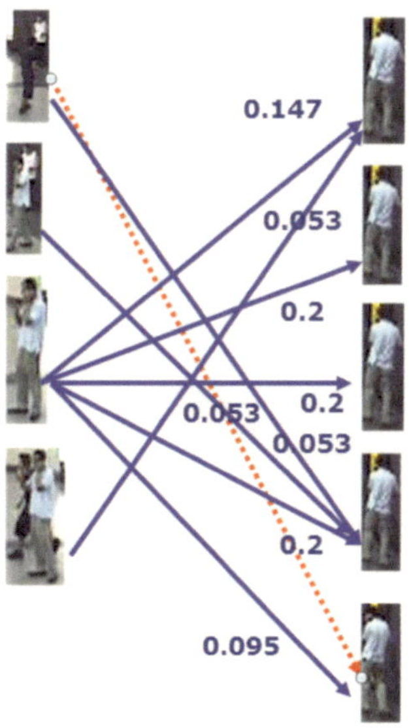

Fig. 12. Hausdorff-based and EMD-based object matching methods. Hausdorff-based object matching is determined by the distance between blob 1 of object Oq and blob 5 of object O_p (dot line) while EMD-based object matching search for an optimal solution.

With the output of the second object signature building approach, the object matching is relatively simple.

4. Surveillance object retrieval results

4.1 Databases

Despite the fact that a number of surveillance video systems have been deployed, very few surveillance databases are available. One reason is that surveillance videos concern to human and organization privacy. Recently, several surveillance video databases such as CAVIAR, i-LIDS, CARETAKER have been released for research purpose. CAVIAR (Context Aware Vision using Image-based Active Recognition) is a project funded by the EC's Information Society Technology's programme project IST 2001 37540. This project addresses two surveillance applications: city centre surveillance and marketers. Corresponding to these applications, two databases are available. Video clips in the first database were filmed with a wide angle camera lens in the entrance lobby of the INRIA Labs at Grenoble (France) while those of the second database are filmed with a wide angle lens along and across the hallway in a shopping centre in Lisbon (Portugal). Moreover, videos of these databases are annotated. 2008 i-LIDS Multiple-Camera Tracking Scenario (MCTS) is a data set with multiple camera views from a busy airport arrival hall (Zheng, Gong et al. 2009). In the context of CARETAKER (Content Analysis and REtrieval Technologies to Apply Extraction to massive Recording), a video surveillance database is available. This project aims at studying, developing and assessing multimedia knowledge-based content analysis, knowledge extraction components and meta data management sub-systems in the context of automated situation awareness, diagnosis and decision support. During this project, a real testbed sites inside the metro of Roma and Torin, involving more than 30 sensors (20 cameras and 10 microphones) have been provided.

4.2 Surveillance object retrieval results

In recent years, a number of surveillance video retrieval results have been published. However, with the lack of common benchmarks and databases, the comparison of these results is difficult (even impossible). Two preliminary comparisons of three object signature building and object matching methods with CAVIAR and CARETAKER dataset have been presented in (Le, Thonnat et al. 2009a) (Le, Thonnat et al. 2009). However, these comparisons are done with a relatively small dataset.

5. Conclusions

In this chapter, firstly a brief overview of surveillance object retrieval is given. Then, current work dedicated to appearance-based surveillance object retrieval are analysed in detail. The analysis shows that preliminary and promising results have been obtained for surveillance object retrieval. However, it is still a challenging issue. This issue needs more work and contributions on surveillance video analysis, feature extraction and common benchmark for surveillance object retrieval evaluation.

6. References

Bak, S., E. Corvee, et al. (2010). Person Re-identification Using Spatial Covariance Regions of Human Body Parts. *AVSS*.

Broilo, M., N. Piotto, et al. (2010). Object Trajectory Analysis in Video Indexing and Retrieval Applications. *Video Search and Mining Studies in Computational Intelligence*, Springer Berlin Heidelberg. 287: 3–32.

Buchin, M., A. Driemel, et al. (2010). An Algorithmic Framework for Segmenting Trajectories based on Spatio-Temporal Criteria. *18th ACM SIGSPATIAL Int. Conf. Advances in Geographic Information Systems (ACM GIS)*.

Calderara, S., R. Cucchiara, et al. (2006). Multimedia Surveillance: Content-based Retrieval with Multicamera People Tracking. *ACM International Workshop on Video Surveillance & Sensor Networks (VSSN'06)*. Santa Barbara, California, USA: 95-100.

Chen, L., M. T. Ozsu, et al. (2004). Symbolic Representation and Retrieval of Moving Object Trajectories. *MIR'04*.

Hsieh, J. W., S. L. Yu, et al. (2006). "Motion-Based Video Retrieval by Trajectory Matching." *Proc IEEE Trans. on Circuits and Systems for Video Technology* 16(3).

Hu, W., D. Xie, et al. (2007). "Semantic-Based Surveillance Video Retrieval." *IEEE Transactions on Image Processing* 16(4): 1168–1181.

Le, T.-L., A. Boucher, et al. (2007). *Subtrajectory-Based Video Indexing and Retrieval*. The International MultiMedia Modeling Conference (MMM'07), Singapore.

Le, T.-L., A. Boucher, et al. (2010). *Surveillance video retrieval: what we have already done?* ICCE, Nha Trang, VietNam.

Le, T.-L., M. Thonnat, et al. (2009)a. *Appearance based retrieval for tracked objects in surveillance videos*. ACM International Conference on Image and Video Retrieval 2009 (CIVR 2009), Santorini, Greece.

Le, T.-L., M. Thonnat, et al. (2009). "Surveillance video indexing and retrieval using object features and semantic events." *International Journal of Pattern Recognition and Artificial Intelligence, Special issue on Visual Analysis and Understanding for Surveillance Applications* 23(7): 1439-1476

Ma, Y. and B. M. a. I. Cohen (2007). Video Sequence Querying Using Clustering of Objects' Appearance Models. *International Symposium on Visual Computing (ISVC'07)*: 328–339.

Nghiem, A.-T., F. Bremond, et al. (2007). ETISEO, performance evaluation for video surveillance systems. *In Proceedings of International Conference on Advanced Video and Signal Based Surveillance (AVSS'07)*. London, United Kingdom.

Rubner, Y., C. Tomasi, et al. (1998). A metric for distributions with applications to image databases. *ICCV'98*: 59–66.

Senior, A. (2009). An Introduction to Automatic Video Surveillance *Protecting Privacy in Video Surveillance*: 1-9.

Velipasalar, S., L. M. Brown, et al. (2010). "Detection of user-defined, semantically high-level, composite events, and retrieval of event queries " *Multimedia Tools and Applications* 50(1): 249-278.

Won, C. S., D. K. Park, et al. (2002). "Efficient use of mpeg-7 edge histogram descriptor." *ETRI Journal* 24: 23–30.

Yuk, J. S. C., K. Y. K. Wong, et al. (2007). Object-Based Surveillance Video Retrieval System with Real-Time Indexing Methodology. *International Conference on Image Analysis and Recognition (ICIAR'07)*: 626-637.

Zhang, C., X. Chen, et al. (2009). "Semantic retrieval of events from indoor surveillance video databases." *Pattern Recognition Letters* 30(12): 1067-1076.

4

Quality Assessment in Video Surveillance

Mikołaj Leszczuk, Piotr Romaniak and Lucjan Janowski
AGH University of Science and Technology
Poland

1. Introduction

Anyone who has experienced artifacts or freezing play while watching a film or a live sporting event on TV is familiar with the frustration accompanying sudden quality degradation at a key moment. Notwithstanding, video services with blurred images may have far more severe consequences for video surveillance practitioners. Therefore, the Quality of Experience (QoE) concept for video content used for entertainment differs considerably from the quality of video used for recognition tasks. This is because in the latter case subjective user satisfaction depends only or almost only on the possibility of achieving a given functionality (event detection, object recognition). Additionally, the quality of video used by a human observer for recognitions tasks is considerably different from objective video quality used in computer processing (Computer Vision).

So called, task-based videos require a special framework appropriate to the video's function — i.e. its use for recognition tasks rather than entertainment. Once the framework is in place, methods should be developed to measure the usefulness of the reduced video quality rather than its entertainment value. The precisely computed usefulness can be used to optimize not only the video quality but the whole surveillance system. It is especially important since surveillance systems often aggregates large number of cameras which streams has to be saved for possible future investigation. For example in Chicago at least 10,000 surveillance cameras are connected to a common storing system (ACLU, 2011).

To develop accurate objective measurements (models) for video quality, subjective experiments must be performed. For this purpose, the ITU-T[1] P.910 Recommendation "Subjective video quality assessment methods for multimedia applications" (ITU-T, 1999) addresses the methodology for performing subjective tests in a rigorous manner.

In this chapter the methodology for performing subjective tests is presented. It is shown that subjective experiments can be very helpful nevertheless they have to be correctly prepared and analyzed. For illustration of the problem, license plates recognition analysis is shown in detail.

2. Related work

Some subjective recognition metrics, described below, have been proposed over the past decade. They usually combine aspects of Quality of Recognition (QoR) and QoE. These metrics have been not focused on practitioners as subjects, but rather on naïve participants.

[1] International Telecommunication Union — Telecommunication Standardization Sector

The metrics are not context specific, and they do not apply video surveillance-oriented standardized discrimination levels.

One of the metrics being definitively worth mention is Ghinea's Quality of Perception (QoP) (Ghinea & Chen, 2008; Ghinea & Thomas, 1998). Anyway, the QoP metric does not entirely fit video surveillance needs. It targets mainly video deterioration caused by frame rate (fps), whereas fps not necessarily affects the quality of CCTV and the required bandwidth (Janowski & Romaniak, 2010). The metric has been established for rather low, legacy resolutions, and tested on rather small groups of subjects (10 instead of standardized 24 valid, correlating subjects). Furthermore, a video recognition quality metric for a clear objective of video surveillance context requires tests in fully controlled environment (ITU-T, 2000), with standardized discrimination levels (avoiding ambiguous questions) and with minimized impact of subliminal cues (ITU-T, 2008).

Another metric being worth mention is QoP's offshoot, Strohmeier's Open Profiling of Quality (OPQ) (Strohmeier et al., 2010). This metric puts more stress on video quality than on recognition/discrimination levels. Its application context, being focused on 3D, is also different than video surveillance which requires rather 2D. Like the previous metric, this one also does not apply standardized discrimination levels, allowing subjects to use their own vocabulary. The approach is qualitative rather than quantitative, whereas the latter is preferred by public safety practitioners for e.g. public procurement. The OPQ model is somehow content/subject-oriented, while for video surveillance more generalized metric framework is needed.

OPQ partly utilizes free sorting, as used in (Duplaga et al., 2008) but also applied in the method called Interpretation Based Quality (IBQ) (Nyman et al., 2006; Radun et al., 2008), adapted from (Faye et al., 2004; Picard et al., 2003). Unfortunately, these approaches allow mapping relational, rather than absolute, quality.

Extensive work has been carried out in recent years in the area of consumer video quality, mainly driven by two working groups: VQiPS (Video Quality in Public Safety) (VQiPS, 2011) and VQEG (Video Quality Experts Group) (VQEG, n.d.).

The VQiPS Working Group, established in 2009 and supported by the U.S. Department of Homeland Security's Office for Interoperability and Compatibility, has been developing a user guide for public safety video applications. The goal of the guide is to provide potential public safety video customers with links to research and specifications that best fit their particular application, as such research and specifications become available. The process of developing the guide will have the desired secondary effect of identifying areas in which adequate research has not yet been conducted, so that such gaps may be filled. A challenge for this particular work is ensuring that it is understandable to customers within public safety, who may have little knowledge of video technology (Leszczuk, Stange & Ford, 2011).

In July 2010, Volume 1.0 of the framework document "Defining Video Quality Requirements: A Guide for Public Safety" was released (VQiPS, 2010). This document provides qualitative guidance, such as explaining the role of various components of a video system and their potential impact on the resultant video quality. The information in this document as well as quantitative guidance have started to become available at the VQiPS Website in June 2011 (VQiPS, 2011).

The approach taken by VQiPS is to remain application agnostic. Instead of attempting to individually address each of the many public safety video applications, the guide is based on commonalities between them. Most importantly, as mentioned above, each application consists of some type of recognition task. The ability to achieve a recognition task is impacted by many parameters, and five of them have been selected as being of particular importance. As defined in: (Ford & Stange, 2010), they are:

1. **Usage time-frame.** Specifies whether the video will need to be analyzed in real-time or will be recorded for later analysis.
2. **Discrimination level.** Specifies how fine a level of detail is sought from the video.
3. **Target size.** Specifies whether the anticipated region of interest in the video occupies a relatively small or large percentage of the frame.
4. **Lighting level.** Specifies the anticipated lighting level of the scene.
5. **Level of motion.** Specifies the anticipated level of motion in the scene.

These parameters form what are referred to as generalized use classes, or GUCs. Figure 1 is a representation of the GUC determination process.

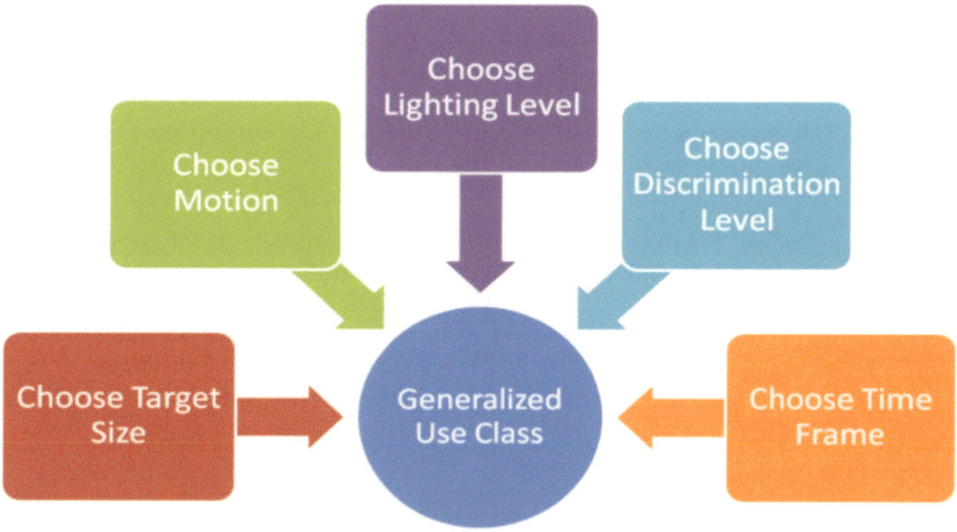

Fig. 1. Classification of video into generalized use classes as proposed by VQiPS (source: (Ford & Stange, 2010)).

The VQiPS user guide is intended to help the end users determine how their application fits within these parameters. The research and specifications provided to users is also to be framed within those parameters. The end user is thus led to define their application within the five parameters and will in turn be led to specifications and other information most appropriate for their needs (Leszczuk, Stange & Ford, 2011).

Recently, a new VQEG project, Quality Assessment for Recognition Tasks (QART), was created for task-based video quality research. QART will address the problems of a lack of quality standards for video monitoring. The aims of QART are the same as the other VQEG projects — to advance the field of quality assessment for task-based video through collaboration in the development of test methods (including possible enhancements of the ITU-T Recommendations), performance specifications and standards for task-based video, and predictive models based on network and other relevant parameters.

3. How it influences the subjective experiment?

The task-based QoE is substantially different from the traditional QoE by different manners. Firstly, as long as a user is able to perform the task we do not have to care if he/she is happy with the overall quality or not up to the level when watching such quality result in fast fatigue of the viewer. Therefore, question about the overall quality does not make much sense. It obviously changes the subjective quality tests significantly.

The second difference between QoE and QoR tests are the source sequences. Let us assume that the task is to recognize if a person on the screen is carrying a gun. In this case more than one source sequence is needed since some alternatives have to be provided. Such alternative sequences have to be very carefully prepared since they should differ from the "gun" sequence by only this one detail. It means that lighting, clouds or any objects at the camera view have to be exactly the same.

The third difference is subjective experiment preparation. In the most traditional QoE experiment a set of parameters of HRC (Hypothetical Reference Circuit) is chosen to produce so called PVS (Processed Video Stream) i.e. a sequence presented to the subjects. A single SRC (Source Reference Circuit) distorted by n different HRCs result in generating n PVSes. In the QoE all those PVSes are shown to a subject so the impact of HRCs can be analyzed. In case of the QoR such methodology is difficult to use. For example in case of plate recognition if a subject recognizes the plates once, he/she can remember them making the next recognition questionable.

Issues of quality measurements for task-based video are partially addressed in the ITU-T P.912 Recommendation "Subjective video quality assessment methods for recognition tasks" (ITU-T, 2008). This Recommendation introduces basic definitions, methods of testing and ways of conducting psycho-physical experiments (e.g. Multiple Choice Method, Single Answer Method, and Timed Task Method), as well as the distinction between Real-Time- and Viewer-Controlled Viewing scenarios. While these concepts have been introduced specifically for task-based video applications in ITU-T P.912, more research is necessary to validate the methods and refine the data analysis methods. In this chapter we present detailed description for which task-based experiments which methodology can be used.

4. What kinds of objective metrics are needed?

In the traditional assessment tests video quality is defined as a satisfaction level of end users, thus QoE. This definition can be generalized over different applications in the area of entertainment. The sources of potential quality degradation are located in different parts of the end-to-end video delivery chain. The first group of distortions can be introduced at the time of image acquisition. The most common problems are noise, lack of focus or improper exposure. Other distortions appear as a result of video compression and processing. Problems can also arise when scaling video sequences in the quality, temporal and spatial domains, as well as, for example, when introducing digital watermarks. Then, for transmission over the network, there may be some artifacts caused by packet loss. At the end of the transmission chain, problems may relate to the equipment used to present video sequences.

In the task-based scenario QoE can be substituted with QoR. The definition of QoR will change along with the specific task requirements and cannot be universally defined. Additionally, subjective answers can be strictly classified as correct or incorrect (i.e. a ground truth is available, e.g. a license plate to be recognized). This is in contradiction to the traditional quality assessment case where there is no ground truth regarding quality.

Because of the above reasons there are additional requirements related to quality metrics. These requirements reflect a specific recognition task but also the viewing scenario. The Real-Time viewing scenario is more similar to the traditional quality assessment tests, although even here additional parameter such as relative target size has to be taken into account. In the case of the Viewer-Controlled viewing scenario additional quality parameters are related to a single shot quality. This is especially important for monitoring objects with a significant velocity. Sharpness of a single video frame (referred to as motion blur) may be a crucial parameter determining the ability to perform a recognition task.

There is one another quality parameter inherent for both viewing scenarios, i.e. source quality of a target. It reflects the ability to perform a given recognition task under the perfect conditions (when additional quality degradation factors do not exist). An example of two similar targets having completely different source quality is two pictures containing car license plate, one taken in a car dealer showroom and one during an off-road race. The second plate may be not only soiled but also blurred due to high velocity of the car. In such a case the license plate source quality is much lower for the second picture what affects significantly recognition ability.

All the additional factors have to be taken into account while assessing QoR for the task-based scenario. The definition of QoR changes between different recognition tasks and requires implementation of dedicated quality metrics.

In the rest of this chapter, as we have already mentioned at the end of Section 1, we would like to review the development of techniques for assessing video surveillance quality. In particular, we introduce a typical usage of task-based video: surveillance video for accurate license plate recognition. Furthermore, we also present the field of task-based video quality assessment from subjective psycho-physical experiments to objective quality models. Example test results and models are provided alongside the descriptions.

5. Case study — License plate recognition test-plan

This section contains a description of the car plate recognition experiment. The purpose of this section is to illustrate an example of a task-based experiment. The presented experiment design phase reveals differences between the traditional QoE assessment and the task-based quality assessment tests. In the following sections, issues concerning the validation of testers and the development of objective metrics are presented.

5.1 Design of the experiment

The purpose of the tests was to analyze the people's ability to recognize car license plates on video material recorded using a CCTV camera and compressed with the H.264/AVC codec. In order to perform the analysis, we carried out a subjective experiment.

The intended outcome of this experiment was to gather the results of the human recognition capabilities. Non-expert testers rated video sequences influenced by different compression parameters. We recorded the video sequences used in the test at a parking lot using a CCTV camera. We adjusted the video compression parameters in order to cover the recognition ability threshold. We selected ITU's ACR (Absolute Category Rating, described in ITU-T P.910 (ITU-T, 1999)) as the applied subjective test methodology.

The recognition task was threefold: 1) type-in the license plate (number), 2) select a car color, and 3) select a car make. We allowed subjects to control playback and enter full screen mode.

We performed the experiment using diverse display equipment in order to be eventually able to analyze the influence of display resolution on the recognition results.

We decided that each tester would score 32 video sequences. The idea was to show each source (SRC) sequence processed under different conditions (HRC) only once and then add two more sequences in order to find out whether testers would remember the license plates already viewed. We screened the n-th tester with two randomly selected sequences and 30 SRCs processed under the following HRCs:

$$\mathrm{HRC} = mod(n - 2 + \mathrm{SRC}, 30) + 1 \tag{1}$$

The tests were conducted using a Web-based interface connected to a database. We gathered

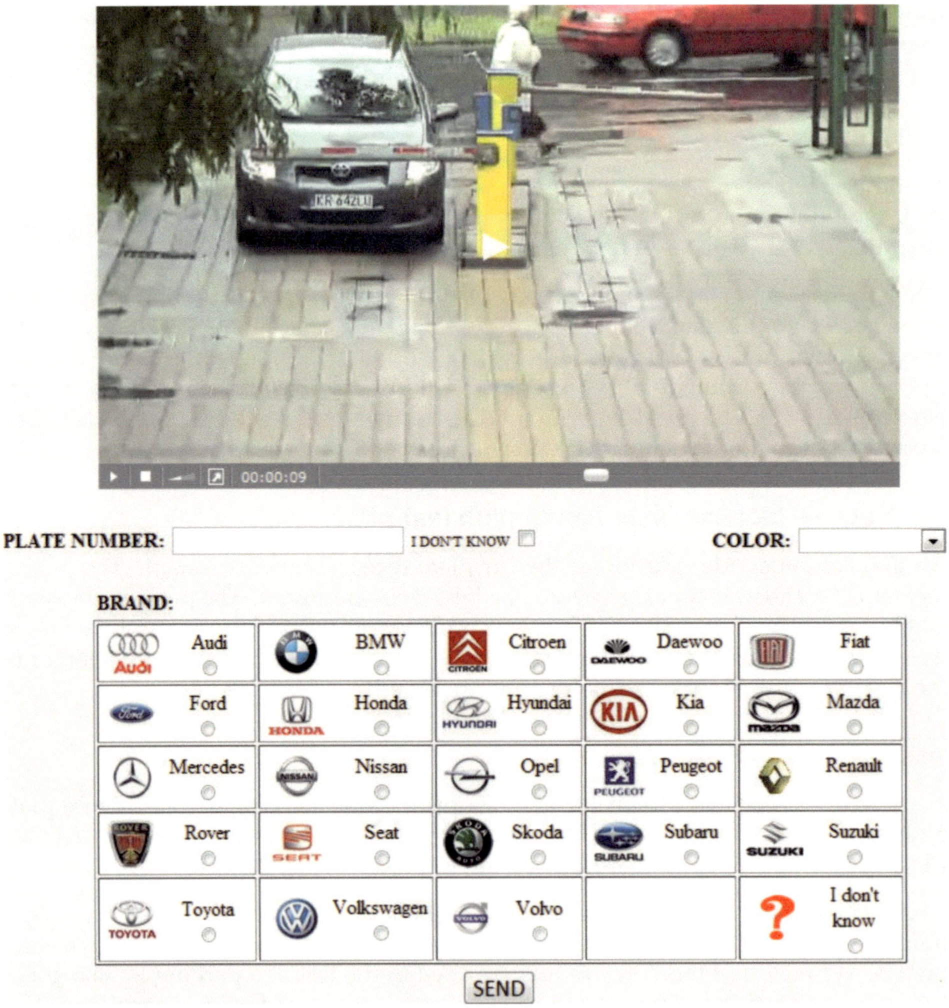

Fig. 2. Test interface.

both information about the video samples and the answers received from the subjects in the database. The interface is presented in Figure 2 (Leszczuk, Janowski, Romaniak, Glowacz & Mirek, 2011).

5.2 Source video sequences

We collected source video sequences at AGH University of Science and Technology in Krakow by filming a car parking lot during high traffic volume. In this scenario, we located the camera 50 meters from the parking lot entrance in order to simulate typical video recordings. Using ten-fold optical zoom, we obtained 6m×3.5m field of view. We placed the camera statically without changing the zoom throughout the recording time, which reduced global movement to a minimum.

We conducted acquisition of video sequences using a 2 mega-pixel camera with a CMOS sensor. We stored the recorded material on an SDHC memory card inside the camera.

We analyzed all the video content collected in the camera and we cut it into 20 second shots including cars entering or leaving the car park. The license plate was visible for a minimum 17 seconds in each sequence. The parameters of each source sequence are as follows:

- resolution: 1280×720 pixels (720p)
- frame rate: 25 frames/s
- average bit-rate: 5.6 — 10.0 Mbit/s (depending on the local motion amount)
- video compression: H.264/AVC in Matroska Multimedia Container (MKV)

We asked the owners of the vehicles filmed for their written consent, which allowed the use of the video content for testing and publication purposes.

5.3 Processed video sequences

If picture quality is not acceptable, the question naturally arises of how it happens. As we have already mentioned at the beginning of Section 5.2, the sources of potential problems are located in different parts of the end-to-end video delivery chain. The first group of distortions (1) can be introduced at the time of image acquisition. The most common problems are noise, lack of focus or improper exposure. Other distortions (2) appear as a result of further compression and processing. Problems can also arise when scaling video sequences in the quality, temporal and spatial domains, as well as, for example, the introduction of digital watermarks. Then (3), for transmission over the network, there may be some artifacts caused by packet loss. At the end of the transmission chain (4), problems may relate to the equipment used to present video sequences.

Considering this, we encoded all source video sequences (SRC) with a fixed quantization parameter QP using the H.264/AVC video codec, x264 implementation. Prior to encoding, we applied some modifications involving resolution change and crop in order to obtain diverse aspect ratios between car plates and video size (see Figure 3 for details related to processing). We modified each SRC into 6 versions and we encoded each version with 5 different quantization parameters (QP). We selected three sets of QPs: 1) $\{43, 45, 47, 49, 51\}$, 2) $\{37, 39, 41, 43, 45\}$, and 3) $\{33, 35, 37, 39, 41\}$. We adjusted selected QP values to different video processing paths in order to cover the license plate recognition ability threshold. We have kept frame rates intact as, due to inter-frame coding, their deterioration does not necessarily result in bit-rates savings (Janowski & Romaniak, 2010). Furthermore, we have not considered network streaming artifacts as we believed that in numerous cases they are related to excessive bit-streams, which we had already addressed by different QPs. Reliable video streaming solution should adjust video bit-stream according to the available network resources and prevent from packet loss. As a result, we obtained 30 different HRC.

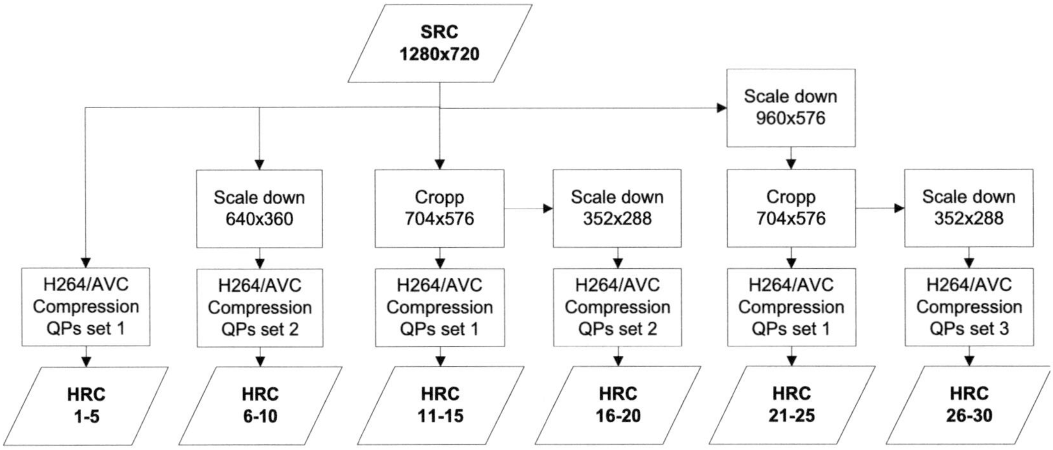

Fig. 3. Generation of HRCs.

Based on the above parameters, it is easy to determine that the whole test set consists of 900 sequences (each SRC 1-30 encoded into each HRC 1-30).

6. Testers' validation

One of the problems with each subjective experiments is reliability of the subjects, or, more precisely, of each individual subject. If a subject proves to be unreliable, any conclusions based on his/her answers may be misleading or simply useless. Therefore the issue of detecting and eliminating unreliable subjects is important in all types of subjective experiments.

Eliminating subjects needs to be based on strict rules, otherwise there is a risk that a subject is eliminated simply because his/her answers do not fit the theory being tested. In other words, any subjective criteria need to be eliminated. The correct methodology should be objective and allow for each subject's individual preferences.

On the other hand, it is necessary to detect subjects who do not take the experiment seriously, i.e. they answer randomly and do not care about giving correct and precise answers. There may also be subjects for whom a given test is too difficult (for example video sequences appear too fast).

The most popular way to validate subjects is correlation. It is a simple and intuitively correct method. We compute correlation between individual subject scores and the scores for all other subjects. We used this method in VQEG in (VQE, 2010). The problems entailed in are: (1) setting the subject elimination threshold (2) eliminating subjects no single answers, and (3) all subjects need to carry out the same tasks numerous times. For the first problem, an experienced scientist can specify correct threshold fitting the problem which he/she is analyzing. The second problem is more difficult to deal with. We know that even for reliable subjects some of their answers are likely to be incorrect. This may be a simple consequence of being tired or distracted for a short period of time. Correlation methodology cannot help in dealing with this problem. The third problem is not important for quality based subjective experiments, since the same sequences are scored in any case (e.g. the same source sequence encoded using different compression parameters). Nevertheless, in task-based subjective experiments the same source sequence should not be shown many times, because the correct answer for a particular task could be remembered. For this reason different pool of sequences is shown to different subjects (e.g. each compression level for a given source sequences needs to be shown to a different subject).

A more formal way toward validation of subjects is the Rasch theory (Boone et al., 2010). It defines the difficult level for each particular question (e.g. single video sequence from a test set), or whether a subject is more or less critical in general. Based on this information it is possible to detect answers that not only do not fit the average, but also individual subjects' behavior. Formally the probability of giving correct answer is estimated by equation (Baker, 1985)

$$P(X_{in} = 1) = \frac{1}{1 + \exp(\beta_n - \delta_i)} \quad (2)$$

where β_n is ability of nth person to make a task and δ_i is the ith task difficulty.

Estimating both the task difficulty and subject ability make it possible to predict the correct answer probability. Such probability can be compared with the real task result.

In order to estimate β_n and δ_i values the same tasks have to be run by all the subjects which is a disadvantage of the Rasch theory, similarly to the correlation-based method. Moreover, the more subjects involved in the test, the higher the accuracy of the method. An excellent example of this methodology in use is national high school exams, where the Rasch theory helps in detecting the differences between different boards marking the pupils' tests (Boone et al., 2010). In subjective experiments, there are always limited numbers of answers per question. This means that the Rasch theory can still be used, although the results need to be checked carefully. Tasks-based experiments are a worst-case scenario. In this case each subject carries out a task a very limited number of times in order to ensure that the task result (for example license plate recognition) is based purely on the particular distorted video and is not remembered by the subject. This makes the Rasch theory difficult to use.

In order to solve this problem we propose two custom metrics for subject validation. They both work for partially ordered test sets (Insall & Weisstein, 2011), i.e. those for which certain subsets can be ordered by task difficulty. Additionally we assume that answers can be classified as correct or incorrect (i.e. a ground truth is available, e.g. a license plate to be recognized). Note that due to the second assumption these metrics cannot be used for quality assessment tasks, since we cannot say that one answer is better than another (as we have mentioned before, there is no ground truth regarding quality).

6.1 Logistic metric

Assuming that the test set is partially ordered can be interpreted in a numeric way: if a subject fails to recognize a license plate, and for n sequences with higher or equal QP the license plate was recognized correctly by other subjects, the subject's inaccuracy level is increased by n. Higher n values may indicate a better chance that the subject is irrelevant and did not pay attention to the recognition task.

Computing such coefficients for different sequence results in the total subject quality (Sq_i) given by

$$Sq_i = \sum_{j \in S_i} ssq_{i,j} \quad (3)$$

where S_i is set of all sequences carried out by ith subject, and $ssq_{i,j}$ is the subject sequence quality for sequence j, which is given by

$$ssq_{i,j} = \begin{cases} 0 \text{ if } r(i,j) = 1 \\ n \text{ if } r(i,j) = 0 \end{cases} \quad (4)$$

where

$$n = \sum_{k \in A_j} \sum_{m \in B} r(m,k) \quad (5)$$

where $r(i,j)$ is 1 if ith subject recognized the jth sequence and 0 otherwise, B is set of all subjects, and A_j is a set of all not easier sequences as defined above. In the case of this experiment A_j is a set of sequences with the same resolution and view although with a higher or equal QP than the jth sequence.

We computed Sq for each subject; the results are presented in Figure 4.

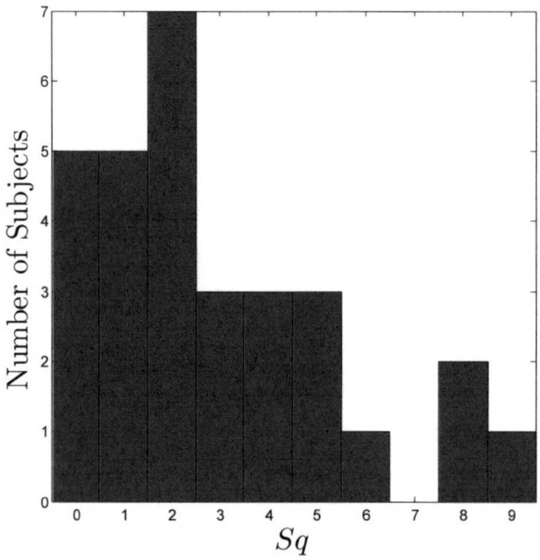

Fig. 4. Histogram of subject quality Sq obtained for all 30 subjects.

The histogram shows that the value of 6 was exceeded for just three subjects, denoted with IDs 18, 40 and 48. Such subjects should be removed from the test.

Sq_i metric assumes that a task can be done correctly or incorrectly. In case of recognition missing one character or all characters the metric returns the same value. In case of license plate recognition and many other tasks the level of error can be defined. The next proposed metric takes into consideration to incorrectness level of the answer.

6.2 Levenshtein distance

Levenshtein distance is the number of edits required to obtain one string from another. Subject quality based on Levenshtein distance Sql is given by

$$Sql_i = \sum_{j=1}^{30} ssql_{i,j} \quad (6)$$

where $ssql_{i,j}$ is subject quality metric based on Levenshtein distance obtained for subject i and sequence j given by

$$ssql_{i,j} = \sum_{k \in A_j} \sum_{m \in B} \begin{cases} 0 & \text{if } l(i,j) \leq l(m,k) \\ l(i,j) - l(m,k) & \text{if } l(i,j) > l(m,k) \end{cases} \tag{7}$$

where $l(i,j)$ is the Levenshtein distance between the correct answer and the subject i answer for the jth sequence, B is set of all subjects, and A_j is the set of all sequences for which the task is not easier defined at the beginning of the section.

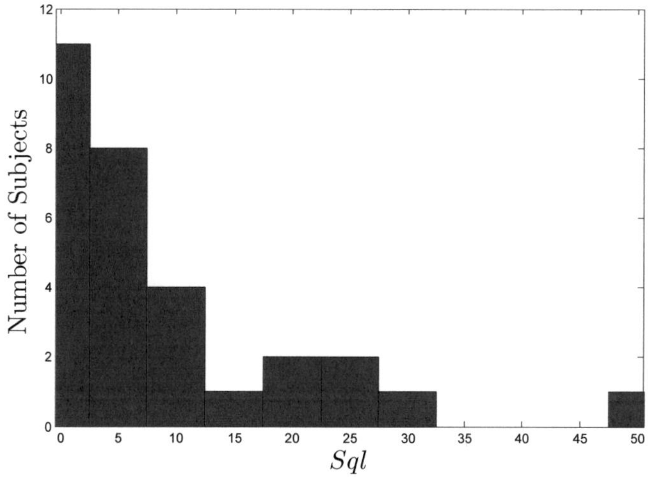

Fig. 5. Histogram of subject quality Sql obtained for all 30 subjects.

Figure 5 shows the histogram obtained for Sql. It is significantly different than the previous one obtained for Sq. It can be assumed that an Sql higher than 10 or 15 indicates a potentially irrelevant subject. One subject obtained significantly higher Sql value than the others (50). More detailed investigation of this case revealed that the subject provided additional text for one answer. After correction the corrected value for this subject is 25, which is still very high.

7. Modeling approaches

In the area of entertainment video, a great deal of research has been carried out on the parameters of the contents that are the most effective for perceptual quality. These parameters form a framework in which predictors can be created such that objective measurements can be developed through the use of subjective testing (Takahashi et al., 2010).

Analysis of the traditional QoE subjective experiment data is focused on the mean subject answer modeling. In addition subject reliability is controlled by the correlation test. Nevertheless, in case of the task-based QoE (QoR) it is impossible or very difficult to use such methodology. Therefore, modeling QoR subjective data calls for new methodology which is presented in this section.

The first step of the subjective experiment data analysis is subject evaluation which is presented in the previous section. The next step of the data analysis is finding the probability of doing a particular task correctly. Again it is different from traditional QoE since the model has to predict probability not the mean value. It calls to use more general models like Generalized Linear Model (GLZ) (Agresti, 2002.).

The last open problems are explanatory variables i.e. the metrics which can correlate well with the probability of the correct task execution. Assessment principles for task-based video quality are a relatively new field. Solutions developed so far have been limited mainly to optimizing network Quality of Service (QoS) parameters. Alternatively, classical quality models such as the Peak Signal-to-Noise Ratio (PSNR) Eskicioglu & Fisher (1995) or Structural Similarity (SSIM) (Wang et al., 2004) have been applied, although they are not well suited to the task. The chapter presents an innovative, alternative approach, based on modeling detection threshold probabilities.

The testers who participated in this study provided a total of 960 answers. Each answer could be interpreted as the number of per-character errors, i.e. 0 errors meaning correct recognition. The average probability of a license plate being identified correctly was **54.8%** (**526/960**), and **64.1%** recognitions had no more than one error. **72%** of all characters was recognized.

7.1 Answers analysis

The goal of this analysis is to find the detection probability as a function of a certain parameter(s) i.e. the explanatory variables. The most obvious choice for the explanatory variable is bit-rate, which has two useful properties. The first property is a monotonically increasing amount of information, because higher bit-rates indicate that more information is being sent. The second advantage is that if a model predicts the needed bit-rate for a particular detection probability, it can be used to optimize the network utilization.

Moreover, if the network link has limited bandwidth the detection probability as a function of a bit-rate computes the detection probability, what can be the key information which could be crucial for a practitioner to decide whether the system is sufficient or not.

The Detection Probability (DP) model should predict the DP i.e. the probability of obtaining 1 (correct recognition). In such cases, the correct model is logit (Agresti, 2002.). The simplest logit model is given by the following equation:

$$p_d = \frac{1}{1 + \exp(a_0 + a_1 x)} \tag{8}$$

where x is an explanatory variable, a_0 and a_1 are the model parameters, and p_d is detection probability.

The logit model can be more complicated; we can add more explanatory variables, which may be either categorical or numerical. Nevertheless, the first model tested was the simplest one.

Building a detection probability model for all of the data is difficult, and so we considered a simpler case based on the HRCs groups (see section 5.3). Each five HRCs (1-5, 6-10, etc.) can be used to estimate the threshold for a particular HRCs group. For example, in Figure 6(a) we show an example of the model and the results obtained for HRCs 20 to 25.

The obtained model crosses all the confidence intervals for the observed bit-rates. The saturation levels on both sides of the plot are clearly visible. Such a model could successfully be used to investigate detection probability.

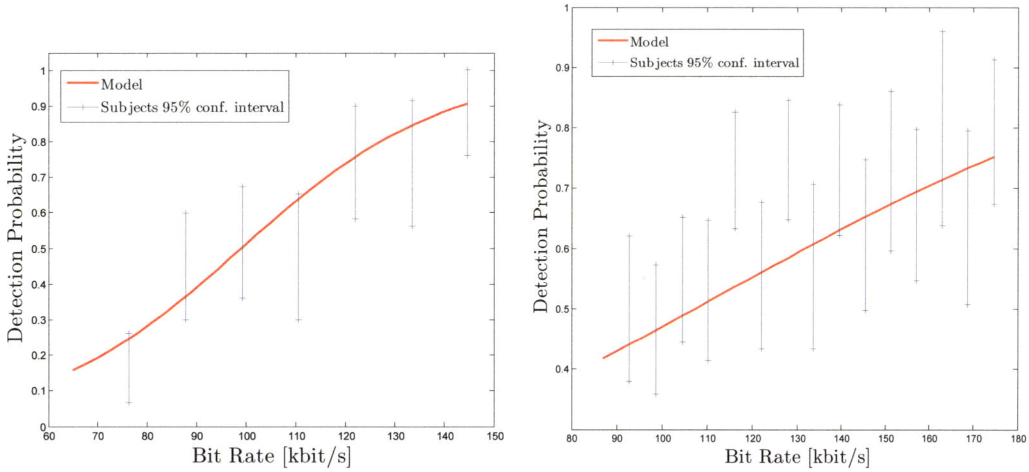

(a) For HRC 20 to 25.

(b) For all HRCs.

Fig. 6. Example of the logit model and the obtained detection probabilities.

We present an extension of the sequences analyzed to all HRCs results in the model drawn in Figure 6(b).

The result obtained is less precise. Some of the points are strongly scattered (see results for bit-rate 110 to 130 kbit/s). Moreover, comparing the models presented in Figure 6(a) and Figure 6(b) different conclusions can be drawn. For example, 150 kbit/s results in around a 90% detection probability for HRCs 20 to 25 and less than 70% for all HRCs. It is therefore evident that the bit-rate itself cannot be used as the only explanatory variable. The question then is, what other explanatory variables can be used.

In Figure 8(a) we show DP obtained for SRCs. The SRCs had a strong impact on the DP. We would like to stress that there is one SRC (number 26) which was not detected even once (see Figure 7(a)). The non-zero confidence interval comes from the corrected confidence interval computation explained in (Agresti & Coull, 1998). In contrast, SRC number 27 was almost always detected, i.e. even for very low bit-rates (see Figure 7(b)). A detailed investigation shows that the most important factors (in order of importance) are:

1. the contrast of the plate characters,
2. the characters, as some of them are more likely to be confused than others, as well as
3. the illumination, if part of the plate is illuminated by a strong light.

A better DP model has to include these factors. On the other hand, these factors cannot be fully controlled by the monitoring system, and therefore these parameters help to understand what kind of problems might influence DP in a working system. Factors which can be controlled are described by different HRCs. In Figure 8(b) we show the DP obtained for different HRCs.

For each HRC, we used all SRCs, and therefore any differences observed in HRCs should be SRC independent. HRC behavior is more stable because detection probability decreases for higher QP values. One interesting effect is the clear threshold in the DP. For all HRCs groups two consecutive HRCs for which the DPs are strongly different can be found. For example, HRC 4 and 5, HRC 17 and 18, and HRC 23 and 24. Another effect is that even for the same QP the detection probability obtained can be very different (for example HRC 4 and 24).

(a) One SRC (number 26) which was not detected even once.

(b) SRC number 27 was almost always detected, i.e. even for very low bit-rates.

Fig. 7. The SRCs had a strong impact on the DP.

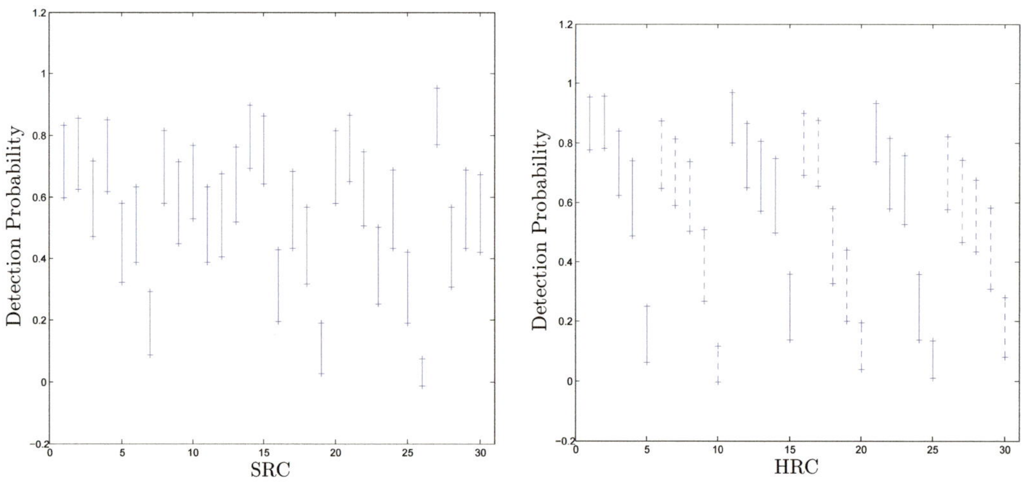

(a) For different SRCs with 90% confidence intervals.

(b) For different HRCs. The solid lines correspond to QP from 43 to 51, and the dashed lines correspond to QP from 37 to 45.

Fig. 8. The detection probabilities obtained.

Different HRCs groups have different factors which can strongly influence the DP. The most important factors are differences in spatial and temporal activities and plate character size. We cropped and/or re-sized the same scene (SRC) resulting in a different output video sequence which had different spatial and temporal characteristics.

In order to build a precise DP model, differences resulting from SRCs and HRCs analysis have to be considered. In this experiment we found factors which influence the DP, but we observed an insufficient number of different values for these factors to build a correct model. Therefore, the lesson learned from this experiment is highly important and will help us to design better and more precise experiments in the future.

7.2 Alternative way of modeling perceptual video quality

For further analysis we assumed that the threshold detection parameter to be analyzed is the probability of plate recognition with no more than one error. For detailed results, please refer to Figure 9.

It was possible to fit a polynomial function in order to model quality (expressed as detection threshold probability) of the license plate recognition task. This is an alternative, innovative approach. The achieved R^2 is 0.86 (see Figure 9). According to the model, one may expect 100% correct recognition for bit-rates of minimum around 360 kbit/s and higher. Obviously accuracy of recognition depends on many external conditions and also size of image details. Therefore 100% can be expected only if other conditions are ideal.

Unfortunately, due to relatively high diversity of subjective answers, no better fitting was achievable in either case. However, a slight improvement is likely to be possible by using other curves.

Summarizing presentation of the results for the quality modeling case, we would like to note that a common method of presenting results can be used for any other modeling case. This

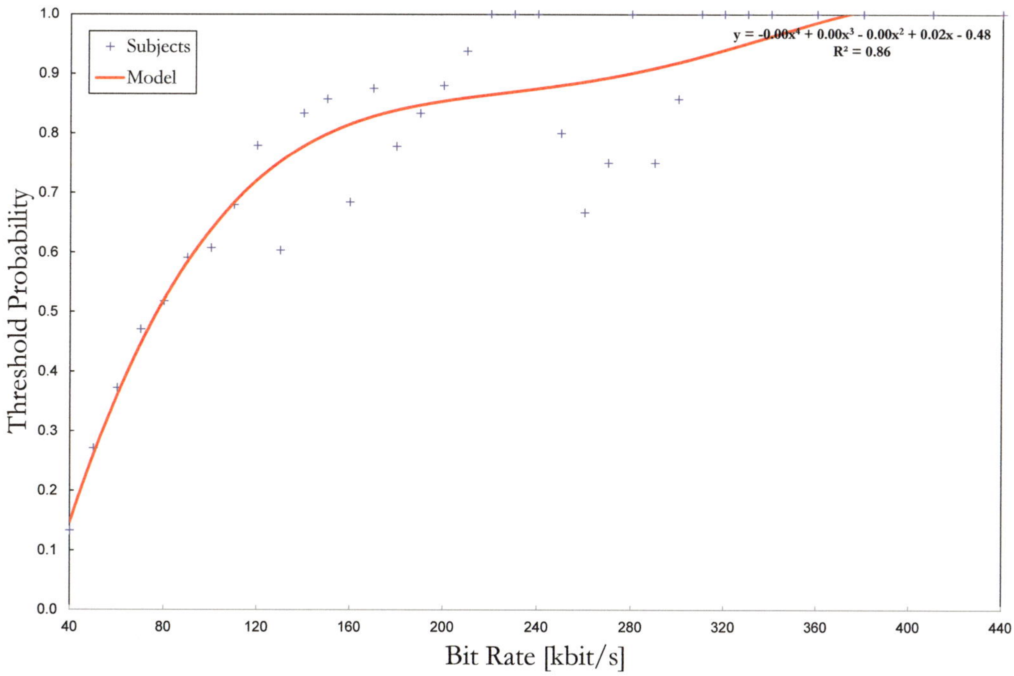

Fig. 9. Example of the obtained detection probability and model of the license plate recognition task.

is possible through the application of appropriate transformations, allowing the fitting of diverse recognition tasks into a single quality framework.

8. Future work

The methodologies outlined in the chapter are just a single contribution to the overall framework of quality standards for task-based video. It is necessary to define requirements starting from the camera, through the broadcast, and until after the presentation. These requirements will depend on scenario recognition.

So far, the practical value of contribution is limited. It refers to limited scenarios. The presented approach is just a beginning of more advanced interesting framework of objective quality assessment, described below (Leszczuk, 2011).

Further steps have been planned in standardization in assessing task-based video quality with relation to QART initiative. Stakeholders list has been initially agreed and action points have been agreed. The plans include: quantifying VQiPS' GUCs, extending test methods (standardization of test methods and experimental designs of ITU-T P.912 Recommendation), measuring camera quality, investigating H.264 encoders, investigating video acuity as well as checking results' stability. The final outcome should be to share ideas on conducting joint experiments and publishing joint papers/VQEG reports, and finally, to submit joint standardization contributions. Plans/next steps for standardizing test methods and experimental designs include verification of issues like: subliminal cues, Computer-Generated Imagery (CGI) source video sequences, automated eye charts as well as subjects' proficiency. The agreed tasks include verifying requirements, refining methods/designs and, finally, making subjective experiments both more accurate and feasible.

9. Acknowledgments

This work was supported by the European Commission under the Grant INDECT No. FP7-218086.

10. References

ACLU (2011). Chicago's video surveillance cameras, *Technical report*, ACLU of Illinois.

Agresti, A. (2002.). *Categorical Data Analysis*, 2nd edn, Wiley.

Agresti, A. & Coull, B. A. (1998). Approximate is better than "exact" for interval estimation of binomial proportions, *The American Statistician* 52(2): 119–126. ISSN: 0003-1305.

Baker, F. B. (1985). *The Basics of Item Response Theory*, Heinemann.

Boone, W. J., Townsend, J. S. & Staver, J. (2010). Using Rasch theory to guide the practice of survey development and survey data analysis in science education and to inform science reform efforts: An exemplar utilizing STEBI self-efficacy data, *Science Education* n/a: 1–23.

Duplaga, M., Leszczuk, M., Papir, Z. & Przelaskowski, A. (2008). Evaluation of quality retaining diagnostic credibility for surgery video recordings, *Proceedings of the 10th international conference on Visual Information Systems: Web-Based Visual Information Search and Management*, VISUAL '08, Springer-Verlag, Berlin, Heidelberg, pp. 227–230.

Eskicioglu, A. M. & Fisher, P. S. (1995). Image quality measures and their performance, *Communications, IEEE Transactions on* 43(12): 2959–2965.
URL: `http://dx.doi.org/10.1109/26.477498`

Faye, P., Br?maud, D., Daubin, M. D., Courcoux, P., Giboreau, A. & Nicod, H. (2004). Perceptive free sorting and verbalisation tasks with naive subjects: an alternative to descriptive mappings, *Food Quality and Preference* 15(7-8): 781 – 791. Fifth Rose Marie Pangborn Sensory Science Symposium. URL: `http://www.sciencedirect.com/science/article/pii/S0950329304000540`

Ford, C. & Stange, I. (2010). A framework for generalising public safety video applications to determine quality requirements, *in* A. Dziech & A. Czyzewski (eds), *Multimedia Communications, Services and Security*, AGH University of Science and Technology Kraków.

Ghinea, G. & Chen, S. Y. (2008). Measuring quality of perception in distributed multimedia: Verbalizers vs. imagers, *Computers in Human Behavior* 24(4): 1317–1329.

Ghinea, G. & Thomas, J. P. (1998). Qos impact on user perception and understanding of multimedia video clips, *Proceedings of the sixth ACM international conference on Multimedia*, MULTIMEDIA '98, ACM, New York, NY, USA, pp. 49–54. URL: `http://doi.acm.org/10.1145/290747.290754`

Insall, M. & Weisstein, E. W. (2011). *Partially Ordered Set*, MathWorld–A Wolfram Web Resource. `http://mathworld.wolfram.com/PartiallyOrderedSet.html`.

ITU-T (1999). Recommendation 910: Subjective video quality assessment methods for multimedia applications, ITU-T Rec. P.910. URL: `http://www.itu.int/`

ITU-T (2000). Recommendation 500-10: Methodology for the subjective assessment of the quality of television pictures, ITU-R Rec. BT.500. URL: `http://www.itu.int/`

ITU-T (2008). Recommendation 912: Subjective video quality assessment methods for recognition tasks, ITU-T Rec. P.912. URL: `http://www.itu.int/`

Janowski, L. & Romaniak, P. (2010). Qoe as a function of frame rate and resolution changes, *in* S. Zeadally, E. Cerqueira, M. Curado & M. Leszczuk (eds), *Future Multimedia Networking*, Vol. 6157 of *Lecture Notes in Computer Science*, Springer Berlin / Heidelberg, pp. 34–45. URL: `http://dx.doi.org/10.1007/978-3-642-13789-1_4`

Leszczuk, M. (2011). Assessing task-based video quality — a journey from subjective psycho-physical experiments to objective quality models, *in* A. Dziech & A. Czyzewski (eds), *Multimedia Communications, Services and Security*, Vol. 149 of *Communications in Computer and Information Science*, Springer Berlin Heidelberg, pp. 91–99. URL: `http://dx.doi.org/10.1007/978-3-642-21512-4_11`

Leszczuk, M. I., Stange, I. & Ford, C. (2011). Determining image quality requirements for recognition tasks in generalized public safety video applications: Definitions, testing, standardization, and current trends, *Broadband Multimedia Systems and Broadcasting (BMSB), 2011 IEEE International Symposium on*, pp. 1 –5.

Leszczuk, M., Janowski, L., Romaniak, P., Glowacz, A. & Mirek, R. (2011). Quality assessment for a licence plate recognition task based on a video streamed in limited networking conditions, *in* A. Dziech & A. Czyzewski (eds), *Multimedia Communications, Services and Security*, Vol. 149 of *Communications in Computer and Information Science*, Springer Berlin Heidelberg, pp. 10–18. URL: `http://dx.doi.org/10.1007/978-3-642-21512-4_2`

Nyman, G., Radun, J., Leisti, T., Oja, J., Ojanen, H., Olives, J. L., Vuori, T. & Hakkinen, J. (2006). What do users really perceive — probing the subjective image quality experience, *Proceedings of the SPIE International Symposium on Electronic Imaging 2006: Imaging Quality and System Performance III, Vol. 6059*, pp. 1–7.

Picard, D., Dacremont, C., Valentin, D. & Giboreau, A. (2003). Perceptual dimensions of tactile textures, *Acta Psychologica* 114(2): 165 – 184. URL: `http://www.sciencedirect.com/science/article/pii/S0001691803000751`

Radun, J., Leisti, T., Häkkinen, J., Ojanen, H., Olives, J.-L., Vuori, T. & Nyman, G. (2008). Content and quality: Interpretation-based estimation of image quality, *ACM Trans. Appl. Percept.* 4: 2:1–2:15. URL: `http://doi.acm.org/10.1145/1278760.1278762`

Strohmeier, D., Jumisko-Pyykkö, S. & Kunze, K. (2010). Open profiling of quality: a mixed method approach to understanding multimodal quality perception, *Adv. MultiMedia* 2010: 3:1–3:17. URL: `http://dx.doi.org/10.1155/2010/658980`

Takahashi, A., Schmidmer, C., Lee, C., Speranza, F., Okamoto, J., Brunnström, K., Janowski, L., Barkowsky, M., Pinson, M., Staelens, Nicolas Huynh Thu, Q., Green, R., Bitto, R., Renaud, R., Borer, S., Kawano, T., Baroncini, V. & Dhondt, Y. (2010). Report on the validation of video quality models for high definition video content, *Technical report*, Video Quality Experts Group.

VQE (2010). *Report on the validation of video quality models for high definition video content*, version 2.0 edn. `http://www.vqeg.org/`.

VQEG (n.d.). The video quality experts group. URL: `http://www.vqeg.org/`

VQiPS (2010). Defining video quality requirements: A guide for public safety, volume 1.0, *Technical report*, U.S. Department of Homeland Security's Office for Interoperability and Compatibility. URL: `http://goo.gl/TJOdU`

VQiPS (2011). Video quality tests for object recognition applications. URL: `http://www.safecomprogram.gov/SAFECOM/library/technology/1627_additionalstatement.htm`

Wang, Z., Lu, L. & Bovik, A. C. (2004). Video quality assessment based on structural distortion measurement, *Signal Processing: Image Communication* 19(2): 121–132. URL: `http://dx.doi.org/10.1016/S0923-5965(03)00076-6%20`

5

Intelligent Surveillance System Based on Stereo Vision for Level Crossings Safety Applications

Nizar Fakhfakh, Louahdi Khoudour,
Jean-Luc Bruyelle and El-Miloudi El-Koursi
French Institute of Science and Technology for Transport, Development and Networks (IFSTTAR)
France

1. Introduction

Considered as a weak point in road and railway infrastructure, level crossings (LC) improvement safety became an important field of academic research and took increasingly railways undertakings concerns. Improving safety of persons and road-rail facilities is an essential key element to ensure a good operating of the road and railway transport. Statistically, nearly 44% of level crossings users have a bad perception of the environment which consequently increases the accidents risks Nelson (2002). However, the behavior of pedestrians, road vehicle drivers and railway operators cannot be previously estimated beforehand. According to Griffioen (2004), the human errors are the causes of 99% of accidents at LC whose 93% are caused by road users. It is important also to note the high cost related to each accident, approximately one hundred million euro per year in the EU for all level crossing accidents. For this purpose, road and railway safety professionals from several countries have been focused on providing a level crossings as safer as possible. Actions are planned in order to exchange information and provide experiments for improving the management of level crossing safety and performance. This has enabled us to discuss sharing knowledge gained from research into improving safety at level crossings.

High safety requirements for level crossing systems mean a high cost which hinders the technological setup of advanced systems. High technology systems are exploited and introduced in order to timely prevent collisions between trains and automobiles and to help reduce levels of risk from railroad crossings. Several conventional object detection systems have been tested on railroad crossings. These techniques provide more or less significant information accuracy. Any proposed system based on a technological solution is not intended to replace the present equipment installed on each level crossing. The purpose of such an intelligent system is to provide additional information to the human operator; it can be considered as support system operations. This concerns the detection and localization of any kind of objects, such as pedestrians, people on two-wheeled vehicle, wheelchairs and car drivers on the dangerous zone Yoda et al. (2006). Today, there are a number of trigger technologies installed at level crossings, but they all serve the same purpose: they detect moving object when passing at particular points in the LC. Indeed, those conventional obstacle detection systems have been used to prevent collisions between trains and automobiles. In Fakhfakh et al. (2010), the conventional technologies applied at LC are discussed and both the advantages and drawbacks of each are highlighted.

One of the main operational purposes for the introduction of CCTV (Closed Circuit Television) at LC is the automatic detection of specific events. Some object detection vision-based systems have been tested at level crossings, and provide more or less significant information. In video surveillance, one camera, or a set of cameras, supervise zones considered as unsafe in which security must be increased Fakhfakh et al. (2011). Referring to the literature, little research has focused on passive vision to solve the problems at LC. Among the existing systems, two of them based on CCTV cameras are to be distinguished: a system using a single camera Foresti (1998). It uses a single grayscale CCD camera placed on a high pole in a corner of the LC, classifying objects as cars, bikes, trucks, pedestrians and others, and localizing them according to the camera calibration process, assuming a planar model of the road and railroad. This system is prone to false and missed alarms caused by fast illumination changes or shadows. In Ohta (2005), a second system using two cameras with a basic stereo matching algorithm and 3D background removal. This system allows detecting more or less vehicles and pedestrians, but it is extremely sensitive to adverse weather conditions. The 3D localization module is not very accurate because of the simplicity of the proposed stereo matching algorithm.

We propose in this chapter an Automatic Video-Surveillance system (AVS) for an automatic detection of specific events at level crossing. The system allows automatically and accurately detecting and 3D localizing obstacles which are stopped or in motion at the level crossing. This information can be timely transmitted to the train's driver, in a form of red lighting in the cabin, and, on his monitor, the images of such hazardous situation. So, we would be able to evaluate the risk and to warn the appropriate persons. This chapter is organized as follows: after an introduction covering the problem and the area of reserach, we describe in section 2 an overview of our proposed system for object localization at LC. Section 3 will focus on detailing the background subtraction algorithm for stationary and moving object detection from real scenes. Section 4 is dedicated to outlining a robust approach for 3D localization the objects highlighted in section 3. Results concern the object extraction and 3D localization steps are detailed in Section 6. The conclusion is devoted to a discussion on the obtained results, and perspectives are provided.

2. Overview of the AVS system

Our research aims at developing an Automatic Video-Surveillance (AVS) system using the passive stereo vision principle. The proposed imaging system uses two color cameras to detect and localize any kind of object lying on a railway level crossing. The system supervises and estimates automatically the critical situations by localizing objects in the hazardous zone defined as the crossing zone of a railway line by a road or path. The AVS system is used to monitor dynamic scenes where interactions take place among objects of interest (people or vehicles). After a classical image grabbing and digitizing step, this architecture is composed of the two following modules:

– *Background Subtraction for Moving and Stationary object detection:* the first step consists in separating the motion and stationary regions from the background. It is performed using Spatio-temporal Independent Component Analysis (stICA) technique for high-quality motion detection. The color information is introduced in the ICA algorithm that models the background and the foreground as statistically independent signals in space and time. Although many relatively effective motion estimation methods exist, ICA is retained for two reasons: first, it is less sensitive to noise caused by the continuously environment changes over time, such as swaying branches, sensor noise, and illumination changes. Second, this method provides clear-cut separation of the objects from the background, and can detect objects that remain motionless for a long period. Foreground extraction is performed separately on both cameras. The motion detection step allows focusing on the areas of interest, in which 3-D localization module is applied.

– *3-D localization of Moving and Stationary object detection:* this process applies a specific stereo matching algorithm for localizing the detected objects. In order to deal with poor quality images, a selective stereo matching algorithm is developed and applied to the moving regions. First, a disparity map is computed for all moving pixels according to a dissimilarity function entitled Weighted Average Color Difference (WACD) detailed in Fakhfakh et al. (2010). An unsupervised classification technique is then applied to the initial set of matching pixels. This allows to automatically choose only well-matched pixels. A pixel is considered as well-matched if the pair of matched pixels have a confidence measure higher than a threshold. The classification is performed applying a Confidence Measure technique detailed in Fakhfakh et al. (2009). It consists in evaluating the result of the likelihood function, based on the *winner-take-all* strategy. However, the disparities of pixels considered as badly-matched are then estimated applying a hierarchical belief propagation technique detailed further. This allows obtaining, for each obstacle, a high accurate dense disparity map.

3. Background subtraction by spatio-temporal independent component analysis

3.1 State of the art

Complex scenes acquired in outdoor environments require advanced tools to be dealt with, for instance, sharp brightness variation, swaying branches, shadows and sensor noise. The use of stationary cameras restricts the choice of techniques to those based on temporal differencing and background subtraction. The latter aims at segmenting foreground regions corresponding to moving objects from the background, somehow by evaluating the difference of pixel features between a reference background and a current scene image. This kind of technique requires updating the background model over time by modeling the possible states that a pixel can take. A trade-off is to be found between performing a real time implementation and handling background changes which are caused by gradual or sudden illumination fluctuations and moving background objects.

The pixel-based techniques assumes statistical independence between the intensity at each pixel throughout the training sequence of images. The main drawback is that it is not effective to model a complex scene. A mixture of Gaussian distribution (GMM) Stauffer & Grimson (2000) have been proposed to model complex and non-static scenes. It consists of modeling the background as a constant or adaptive number of Gaussians. A relatively robust non-parametric method has been proposed in Elgammal et al. (2000). The authors estimate the density function of a distribution given only very recent history information. This method allows obtaining a sensitive detection. In Zhen & Zhenjiang (2008) the authors use an improved GMM and Graph Cut to minimize an energy function to extract foreground objects. The main disadvantage is that the fast variations cannot be accurately modeled.

Another kind of technique, called codebook model, has recently been proposed. It consists in registering, over a long period of time, the possible states of each pixel in what is called a *codebook* Kim et al. (2005) consisting of a set of *codewords*. A pixel is classified into either background or foreground classes by evaluating the difference between a given pixel and the corresponding codebook. A color metric and brightness boundaries are used as criteria for classification. Hence, the existing techniques can handle gradual illumination changes, but remain vulnerable to sudden changes. Several works are mainly focused on how to make foreground object extraction unaffected by background changes. These methods are very sensitive on the background model so that a pixel is correctly classified when a given image is coherent to its corresponding background model. Another issue is in the huge computational time of the background updating process.

In recent years, another kind of technique has emerged to deal with this issue. The Independent Component Analysis (ICA) technique, known for its robustness in the signal processing field, is getting much attention in the image processing field. The purpose of ICA is to restore statistically independent source signals, given only a mixture of these signals. For a short time, ICA is applied to fMRI data by McKeown et al. (1998) and have been then introduced for solving problems related to image processing. Hence, ICA finds applications in many emerging new application areas, such as feature extraction Delfosse & Loubaton (1995), speech and image recognition Cardoso (1997), data communication Oja et al. (1991), sensor signal processing Cvejic et al. (2007) and biomedical signal processing Dun et al. (2007)Waldert (2007).

More recently, ICA has been introduced in video processing to cope with the issue of foreground estimation. Zhang and Chen Zhang & Chen (2006) have introduced a spatio-temporal independent component analysis method (stICA) coupled with multiscale analysis as a postprocessing for automated content-based video processing in indoor environments. Their system is computationally demanding so that the data matrix, from which the independent components must be estimated using ICA, is of a very large dimension. Recently, Tsai and Lai Tsai & Lai (2009) have proposed an ICA model for foreground extraction without background updating in indoor environments. The authors have proposed an algorithm for estimating the de-mixing matrix, which gives the independent components, directly measuring the statistical independence by estimating the joint and marginal probability density functions from relative frequency distributions. But, neither detail of an automated system is proposed. These two related works do not handle the background changes over time and are limited to monochrome images. Furthermore, their algorithms are only tested in indoor environments characterized by small environmental changes.

3.2 Overview of the proposed background subtraction algorithm

The proposed scheme is a complete modelization of the background subtraction task from an image sequence in real-world environments. While considering the acquisition process achieved, the block diagram of the proposed framework is given by Figure 1. The algorithm can be devided into two complementary steps: training step and detection step.

– The first step consists of the estimation of the de-mixing matrix parameter by performing the ICA algorithm on background images only. While any foreground object may appear in the background images, the ICA algorithm allows estimating a source which represents the temporal difference between pixels. Typically, only the five most recent background images seem to be sufficient in our experiments. The matrix which allows separating the foreground from its background, termed de-mixing matrix, is estimated in the following way: the ICA algorithm is performed only once on a data matrix from which the independent components, i.e. the background and the foreground, will be estimated. The data matrix is constructed from two images which are the most recent background, and another on which a foreground object is arbitrarily added. The de-mixing matrix will be used in the detection step.

– The detection step consists of the approximation and the extraction of foreground objects. However, the data matrix is constructed from two images; one is an incoming image from the sequence and the other is the most recent available background. The approximated foreground is then obtained simply by multiplying the data matrix with the de-mixing matrix. The approximated foreground is filtered in order to effectively segment the true foreground objects. This is performed by the use of a spatio-temporal belief propagation method. The principal guidelines of our framework can be explained and summarized in Algorithm 1.

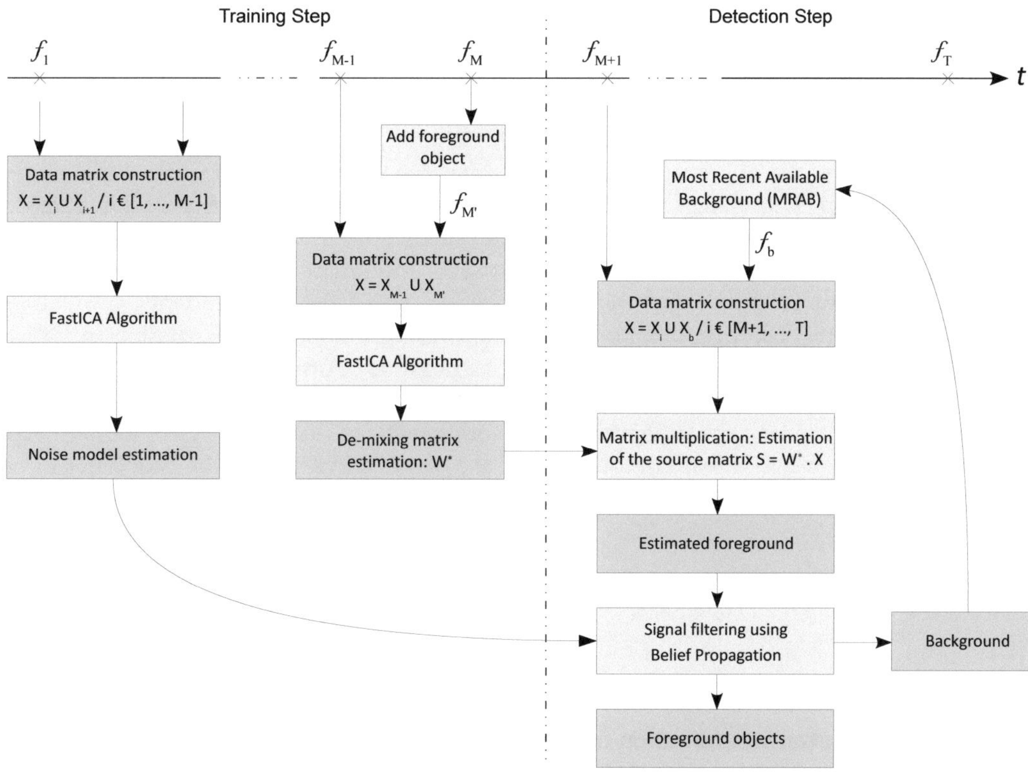

Fig. 1. The block diagram of the proposed background subtraction agorithm.

ICA can be defined as a statistical and computational technique for revealing hidden factors that underlie sets of random variables, measurements or signals. ICA defines a generative

Algorithm 1 Background subtraction for Foreground objects segmentation.

1. Perform the *FastICA* algorithm on a data matrix obtained from two consecutive background images for noise model estimation. The noise model, obtained from the k previous frame, corresponds to the mean and the standard deviation of each color component.

2. Excecute the *FastICA* algorithm only once in order to estimate the de-mixing matrix. The data matrix, from which the *FastICA* algorithm is performed, is constructed of two images: the one corresponds to the background and the other corresponds to the background on which a foreground object is added.

3. Construct the data matrix for foreground approximation. The data matrix is composed of the Most Recent Available Background and an incoming image from the sequence.

4. The approximated foreground is obtained by multiplying the data matrix with the de-mixing matrix obtained from step 2.

5. Filtering of the estimated foreground by the use of a spatio-temporal belief propagation.

model for separating the observed multivariate data that are mixtures of unknown sources without any previous knowledge. It aims to find the source signals from observation data. In that model, the observed data are assumed to be linear mixtures of some unknown latent variables, and the mixing system is also unknown. The latent variables are assumed to be non-Gaussian and mutually independent; they are called the independent components of the observed data. The problem boils down to finding a linear representation in which the components are as statistically independent as possible. Formally, the data are usually represented by a matrix X, the unknown separated source signals by $\tilde{S}$ and the unknown matrix that allow obtaining the independent components by $\tilde{A}$. Thus, every component, say $\tilde{s}_{i,t}$ from $\tilde{S}$, is expressed as linear combination of the observed variables, the problem can be reformulated as Equation 1:

$$X = \tilde{A} \times \tilde{S} \tag{1}$$

After estimating the matrix A, its inverse, called W, can be computed for obtaining the independent components. The model becomes:

$$\tilde{S} = \tilde{A}^{-1} \times X = \tilde{W} \times X \tag{2}$$

3.3 Proposed background subtraction using ICA model

We explain in this section the different parts of our proposed model and how the *FastICA* algorithm is performed for solving ICA model. The number of independent components to be estimated are the two following components: the background and the foreground. Moreover, these two components are assumed to be independent. Indeed, the presence of motion is characterized by a high variation of the intensity of a given pixel. It is to be noted that the presence of an arbitrary foreground object over a background is an independent phenomenon. That is, the intensity of a pixel in a foreground object does not depend on the intensity of its corresponding background.

To begin with, we formulate a video sequence as a set $\mathcal{I}$ of sequential images. An image captured at time t is termed I_t, where $t = 1, \ldots, T$, T is the number of frame in the sequence and $\mathcal{I} = \bigcup_{t \in T} I_t$. We extend the ICA model to exploit the color information for video objects extraction. Each image I_t is a matrix of size $K = h \times w$, where h and w are respectively the height and the width of the image. An observation, noted $I_{p,t}$, corresponds to a pixel sample at location $p = (i, j)$ at time t. Knowing that the color information is considered in the design of our framework, we introduce the parameter c which represents a component of a color space or a normalized color space. For instance, c means either the Red, Green or Blue component in the RGB color space, i.e. $\mathbb{R}^3$. For reasons of simplicity, c^i means one component in the RGB color space where c^1 means the Red, c^2 means the Green and c^3 means the Blue. The data matrix, termed X, is a matrix of two lines and $w \times h \times 3$ columns. To fit the data matrix, each color component of the image I^c at time t is resized to be a column vector of size $h \times w$. Each line of the matrix X is a column vector, V, consisting of the three adjaxent color components $V_k = \langle I_k^{c^1}, I_k^{c^2}, I_k^{c^3} \rangle_t$, where $k \in \{bg, bg + ob\}$ so that the first line represents the background image while the second line represents an image having an arbitrary foregrounds. bg and $bg + ob$ correspond to the background, and the the background on which an object is added. The estimated de-mixing matrix W is a 2-by-2 square matrix and the estimated sources signals $\tilde{S}$ has the same size as the data matrix X. The matrix X obtained at time t is given as follows:

$$X = \begin{pmatrix} V_{bg} \\ V_{bg+ob} \end{pmatrix}_t = \begin{pmatrix} I_{bg}^{c^1}, & I_{bg}^{c^2}, & I_{bg}^{c^3} \\ I_{bg+ob}^{c^1}, & I_{bg+ob}^{c^2}, & I_{bg+ob}^{c^3} \end{pmatrix}_t \quad (3)$$

3.3.1 Foreground approximation

The *FastICA* algorithm is performed only once for initializing the detection process which allows estimating the de-mixing matrix. The data matrix in the detection step is constructed in a different way from that of the training step. The data matrix is formed by both an image containing only the recent background image in the sequence, and another image containing an arbitrary foreground object, if any. The estimated source images correspond to the separated background and only foreground: the one represents only the background source and the other highlights the foreground object, without the detailed contents of the reference background. Figure 2 illustrates the inputs and outputs of the algorithm. The estimated de-mixing matrix will be used to extract the foreground objects from their background during the detection step. In the detection step, the source components are extracted simply by multiplying the data matrix with the estimated de-mixing matrix. Therefore, the data matrix is updated for each incoming image in the sequence in the following way: the second row of the data matrix corresponds to the recent incoming image from the sequence, while the first row corresponds to the Most Recent Available Background (MRAB).

Using this configuration, the two images which constitute the data matrix are not very different because of their temporal proximity. The existing noise among two consecutive images does not degrade the ICA performances and still allows an estimation of the hidden

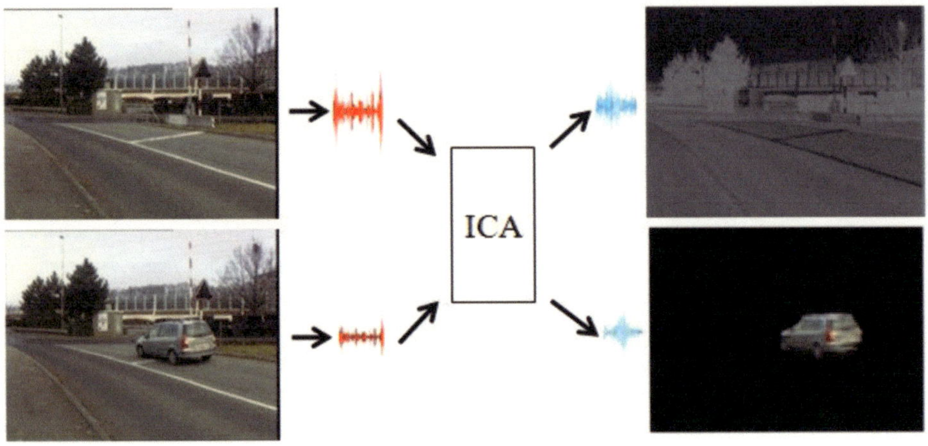

Fig. 2. Principle of the background subtraction using Independent Component Analysis.

sources. The estimated signals are obtained by multiplying the data matrix and the de-mixing matrix.

$$\tilde{S} = \begin{pmatrix} \tilde{V}_{bg} \\ \tilde{V}_{bg+ob} \end{pmatrix} = \begin{pmatrix} w_1 \\ w_2 \end{pmatrix} \times \begin{pmatrix} V_{bg} \\ V_{bg} \end{pmatrix} \tag{4}$$

The first row of the matrix $\tilde{S}$ corresponds to the background model, while the second row represents the estimated foreground signal in which only moving or stationary objects are highlighted. From then on, only the estimated foreground will be taken into account and will be called an "Approximate Foreground". The second row of the matrix $\tilde{S}$ is reshaped from a vector of size $h \times w \times 3$ to a 2D color image of size (h, w) by the linear transformation given by Equation 5:

$$I^c_{i,j,t} = \tilde{S}(1, (l * K) + (i * h) + j) \tag{5}$$

where $c \in \{R, G, B\}$, $K = h \times w$, and l is an integer which takes values 1 if $c = R$, 2 if $c = G$, and 3 if $c = B$. Figure 3 despicts an example of foreground objects extracted by multiplying a de-mixing matrix, estimated using *FastICA* algorithm, and a data matrix formed by the images (a) and (b). The two vectors that form the de-mixing matrix are respectively $w_1 = [0.0285312, 0.0214363]$ and $w_2 = [-0.519938, 0.548299]$. Vector w_1 allows obtaining the estimated background image while vector w_2 allows obtaining the estimated foreground image. Typically, the estimated foreground highlight moving and stationary objects which are smothered by a noisy and uniform background.

The estimated signal is characterized by the presence of zones corresponding to a high intensity variation of the background together with a lot of noise. We have no *a priori* about the noise distribution, making the foreground extraction a task difficult to solve.

3.3.2 Foreground extraction

A. MRF Formulation and Energy Minimization

In this part, we propose a robust framework to accurately extract foreground objects from the estimated foreground signal. This module aims at filtering the estimated foreground by reducing the noise obtained from the ICA model. The problem can be expressed in terms of

(a)

(b)

(c)

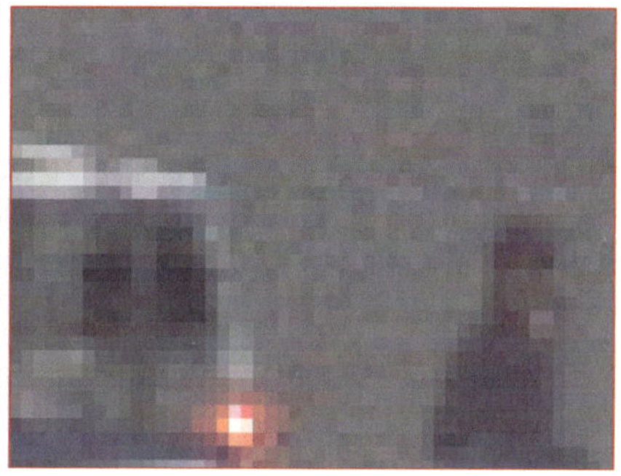

(d)

Fig. 3. Background subtraction and foreground approximation (a) background image from the "Pontet" dataset, (b) scene image from the same dataset containing a car and two pedestrians, (c) estimated foreground image obtained by mutliplying the data matrix, formed by the images (a) and (b), and a de-mixing matrix, where $w_2 = [-0.519938, 0.548299]$, and (d) zooming on a part of a background, a pedestrian and a car that we attempt to separate.

a Markov Random Field (MRF) in which an inference algorithm is applied to find the most likely setting of the model. Several robust inference algorithms such as Graph Cuts and Belief Propagation have emerged and proved their efficiency especially in the realm of stereo Yang et al. (2009) and image restoration Felzenszwalb & Huttenlocher (2006). The formulation we propose aims at clairly separating the foreground from its background by introducing spatial and temporal dependencies between the pixels. The rest of this section will be focused on the spatio-temporal formulation and the algorithm used for minimizing such energy. In what follows, the problem will be formulated as graphical model which consists of an undirected graph on which the inference is performed by approximating the MAP estimate for this MRF using loopy belief propagation. The bipartite graph is denoted by $\mathcal{G} = (\mathcal{P}, E)$ where $\mathcal{P}$ is a set of nodes, i.e. pixels, and E is a set of undirected edges between nodes. Each pixel x is modeled by a state noted $\dot{s}_x$. In computer vision, the edges allow establishing spatial dependencies between nodes. During the message passing procedure, a label is assigned to each node which is the vector of three color components. A state $\dot{s}_x = \langle l_t, \ldots, l_{t-k} \rangle$ of a pixel x is modeled by a vector of labels such as a label l_t corresponds to the color components of pixel p at time t.

Referring to the standard four-connected rectangular lattice configuration, the joint probability of the MRF is given by the product of one- and two-nodes having spatial and temporal dependencies as follows:

$$P(\mathcal{G}) = \prod_{x \in \mathcal{P}} \Phi(\dot{s}_{x(t)}) + \prod_{\substack{x \in \mathcal{P} \\ y \in \mathcal{N}_{s,x}}} \Psi(\dot{s}_{x(t)}, \dot{s}_{y(t)}) + \prod_{x(t-i) \in \mathcal{N}_{t,x}} \Theta(\dot{s}_{x(t)}, \dot{s}_{x(t-i)}) \tag{6}$$

where Φ, Ψ and Θ are functions which describe the dependency between nodes, which will be detailed in section *B*. $\dot{s}_x$ and $\dot{s}_y$ are the state of node x and y respectively, given that y is one of the four spatial neighbors of node x, $\dot{s}_{x(t)}$ is the state of the most recent node x at time t. For a given pixel x, the spatial four-connected nodes form a set of spatial neighboring noted $\mathcal{N}_{s,x}$, and the consecutive temporal neighboring denoted by $\mathcal{N}_{t,x}$. Typically, the optimization is performed by computing the *a posteriori* belief of a variable, which is NP-hard. This has generally been viewed as being too slow to be practical for early vision. The idea is to approximate the optimal solution by inference using belief propagation which is one of the most efficient methods of finding the optimum solution. This allows minimizing the energy function using either the Maximum A Posteriori (MAP) or the Minimum Mean Squared Error (MMSE) estimator.

B. Energy Minimization using Spatio-Temporal Belief Propagation

Intuitively, the objectives can be reformulated, in terms of energy minimization, as the research of the optimal labeling f^* that assigns each pixel $x \in \mathcal{P}$ a label $l \in \mathcal{L}$ by minimizing an energy function. In our case, the energy to minimize is represented as a linear combination of three terms: data term, spatial smoothness term, and temporal filtering term. The data term measures how well state $\dot{s}$ fits pixel x, given its observed data, the spatial smoothness term measures the extent to which the state $\dot{s}$ is not spatially piecewise smooth, and the temporal filtering term evaluates the temporal dependencies of the consecutive states of a pixel x over time by using its known previous optimal labels. Checking both the piecewise spatial smoothness and temporal filtering allows obtaining a robust motion-based classification.

Intuitively, the optimal labeling can be found by maximizing a probability. The MAP estimate is equivalent to minimizing the Equation 6 by taking the negative log, so writing $\phi = -\log \Phi$, $\psi = -\log \Psi$, and $\theta = -\log \Theta$, the objectibe can be reformulated as minimizing the posterior log as a function of the form:

$$E(\mathcal{G}) = \sum_{x \in P} \phi(\dot{s}_{x(t)}) + \sum_{\substack{x \in \mathcal{P} \\ y \in \mathcal{N}_{s,x}}} \psi(\dot{s}_{x(t)}, \dot{s}_{y(t)}) + \sum_{x(t-i) \in \mathcal{N}_{t,x}} \theta(\dot{s}_{x(t)}, \dot{s}_{x(t-i)}) \tag{7}$$

The formulation we consider in our framework consists in optimizing the data term denoted by $E_{data}(\hat{f})$, the spatial smoothness term denoted by $E_{s\_smooth}(\hat{f})$ and the temporal filtering term denoted by $E_{t\_filtering}(\hat{f})$. By treating the problem in the context of filtering, the outputs from previous frames can be incorporated by adding an extra term to the energy function. The Global Energy Minimization function can be formulated as follows:

$$E(\mathcal{G}) = E_{data}(\hat{f}) + E_{s\_smooth}(\hat{f}) + E_{t\_filtering}(\hat{f}) \tag{8}$$

However, Equation 7 can be expressed as:

$$E(\mathcal{G}) = \sum_{x \in P} D_x(\dot{s}_{x(t)}) + \sum_{\substack{x \in \mathcal{P} \\ y \in \mathcal{N}_{s,x}}} V_s(\dot{s}_{x(t)}, \dot{s}_{y(t)}) + \sum_{x(t-i) \in \mathcal{N}_t, x} V_t(\dot{s}_{x(t)}, \dot{s}_{x(t-i)}) \tag{9}$$

– Data term : In stereo problems, data term usually corresponds to the cost of matching a pixel in the left-image to another in the right-image. Typically, this term, i.e. cost, is based on the intensity differences between the two pixels. Just like in this present case, the data term $D_x(\dot{s}_x)$ is defined as the cost of assigning a label l_x to pixel x. It can be expressed as the Euclidean distance between the color components of the pixel x and a given label l_x. In order to control the evolution of the energy function, the data term can be written as:

$$D_x(\dot{s}_x) = \begin{cases} 0 & \text{if } |\dot{s}_{x(t)} - l_x| \leq \varepsilon \\ |\dot{s}_{x(t)} - l_x| & \text{otherwise} \end{cases} \tag{10}$$

where ε is constant. The data term depends only on the parameter α of the state of the node. The rest of parameters are not considered for the computation of this term.

– Spatial smoothness term : The choice of the smoothness term is a critical issue. Several cost terms have been proposed which heavily depend on the problem to be solved. Assuming the pair-wise interaction between two adjacent pixels x and y, the spatial smoothness term can be formulated using the Potts model Wu (1982). This is motivated by the fact that this piecewise smooth model encourages a labeling consisting of several regions where pixels in the same moving region have similar labels. The cost of the spatial smoothness term is given by:

$$V_s(\dot{s}_{x(t)}, \dot{s}_{y(t)}) = \begin{cases} 0 & \text{if } \Delta_{x,y} \leq \xi \\ \Delta_{x,y}.T & \text{otherwise} \end{cases} \tag{11}$$

where $\Delta_{x,y}$ is the Euclidean distance between the two neighboring pixels x and y at the same time, ξ is a constant, and T is the temperature variable of the Potts model which can be estimated appropriately by simulating the Potts model. In our case, we choose to take T as a constant.

– Temporal filtering term Making use of an additional term which represents the temporal filtering in the energy function is very useful for improving the performances of the passing message procedure. The optimal labels obtained for a node during the k previous images are used for quickly reaching the optimal label in the current node at time t. Each current node uses its previous best set of labels obtained for the same node during the k previous images. The temporal filtering term is given by the following:

$$\theta\left(\dot{s}_{x(t)}, \dot{s}_{x(t-i)}\right) = \sum \kappa. \left\| \dot{s}_{x(t)} - \dot{s}_{x(t-i)} \right\| \tag{12}$$

where κ is a binary parameter which takes values 0 or 1. In the case where the most temporally neighboring pixel is classified as a background, the parameter κ is set to 1 for all temporally neighboring pixels which are classified as background, 0 otherwise.

C. Foreground/Background Classification

This final step consists in automatically extracting all foreground objects from their background in the aforementioned filtered foreground image, noted I_f. The classification step is preceded by postprocessing the output color image on which the background is uniform, while all moving and stationary objects are well highlighted. The postprocessing aims at binarizing the image and classifying all pixels into two classes: foreground and background. To this end, the color components $I_f^{c_i}$, where c_i is the ith color component, are extracted from the color image I_f. Then, a Sobel operator *Sob* is applied to each color component which aims at performing a 2-D spatial gradient measurement on an image and so emphasizes regions of high spatial frequency that correspond to edges. For each color component, two edge images are obtained which represent the edges obtained from the horizontal and the vertical directions. The union of these two images forms the V-H (Vertical-Horizontal) edges of the image. Thus, an edge image is obtained for each color component. The final edge image is obtained by intersecting the points of the edges of the three images. The final edges E of the image is obtained as follows.

$$E(I_f^{c_i}) = Sob(I_f^{c_i})_{dx} \cup Sob(I_f^{c_i})_{dy} \tag{13}$$

$$E(T_f) = E(I_f^{c_1}) \cap E(I_f^{c_2}) \cap E(I_f^{c_3}) \tag{14}$$

The final map which contains only moved and stationary onjects is obtained by merging $E(T_f)$ and another map $S(T_f)$. The $S(T_f)$ map is obtained by a color segmentation process applied on the obtained filtering image.

4. 3D localization of obstacles by stereo matching

The use of more than one camera provides additional information, such as the depth of objects in a given scene. Dense or sparse stereovision techniques can be used to match points. When a point is imaged from two different viewpoints, its image projection undergoes a displacement from its position in the first image to that in the second image. Each disparity, determined for each pixel in the reference image, represents the coordinate difference of the projection of a real point in the 3-D space, i.e. scene point, in the left- and right-hand images of the cameras. A depth map is obtained from the two images and, for each disparity, the corresponding real 3-D coordinates are estimated according to the intrinsic and extrinsic parameters, such as the focal length and the baseline. The amount of displacement, alternatively called disparity, is inversely proportional to distance and may therefore be used to compute 3D geometry. Given a correspondence between imaged points from two known viewpoints, it is possible to compute depth by triangulation.

Several well-known stereo algorithms compute an initial disparity map from a pair of images under a known camera configuration. These algorithms are based loosely on local methods, such as window correlation, which take into account only neighborhood points of the pixel to be matched. The obtained disparity map has a lot of noise and erroneous values. This noise concerns mostly the pixels belonging to occluded or textureless image regions. An iterative process is then applied to the initial disparity map in order to improve it. These methods use global primitives. Some research has used a graph-based method Foggia et al. (2007) and color segmentation based stereo methods Taguchi et al. (2008) which belong to what is called *global approaches*. Other approaches have been proposed: they are based on a probabilistic framework optimization, such as belief propagation Lee & Ho (2008). These methods aim to obtain high-quality and accurate results, but are very expensive in terms of processing time. It is a real challenge to evaluate stereo methods in the case of noise, depth discontinuity, occlusions and non-textured image regions.

In our context, the proposed stereo matching algorithm is applied only on moving and stationary zones automatically detected referring to the technique discussed in the previous section. However, costs and processing time are decreasing at a steady pace, and it is becoming realistic to believe that such a thing will be commonplace soon. The stereo algorithm presented further, springs from relaxation and energy minimization fields. Our approach aims to represent a novel framework to improve color dense stereo matching. As a first step, disparity map volume is initialized applying a new local correlation function. After that, a confidence measure is attributed to all the pairs of matched pixels, which are classified into two classes: well-matched pixel and badly-amtched pixel. Then, the disparity value of all badly-matched pixels is updated based only on stable pixels classified as well-matched in an homogeneous color region. The well-matched pixels are used as input into disparity re-estimation modules to update the remaining pixels. The confidence measure is based on a set of original local parameters related to the correlation function used in the first step of our algorithm. This paper will focus on this point. The main goal of our study is to take into account both quality and speed. The global scheme of the stereo matching algorithme we propose is given by figure 4.

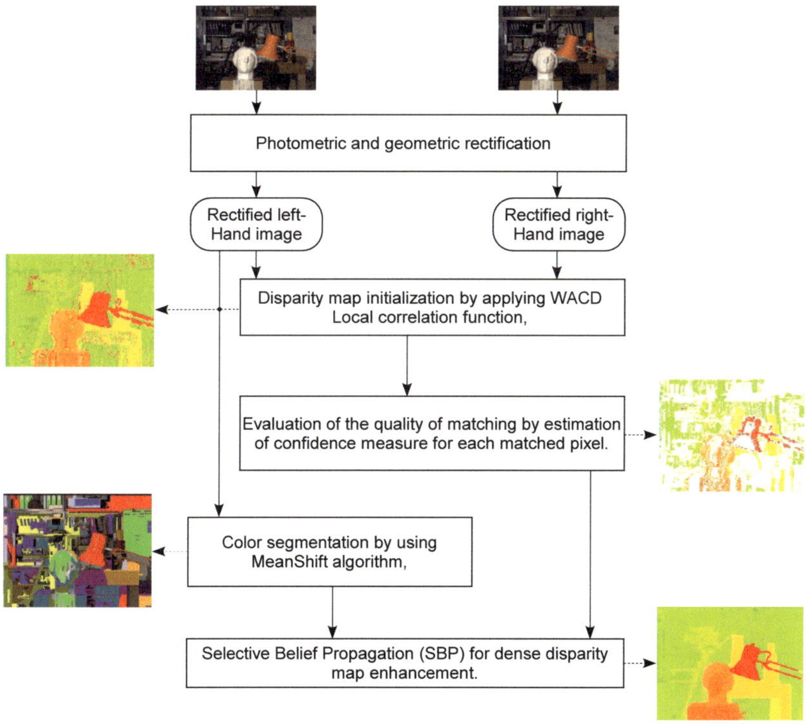

Fig. 4. Global scheme of the stereo matching algorithm for 3D localization.

4.1 Global energy formulation

The global energy to minimize is composed of two terms: data cost and smoothness constraint, noted f and $\hat{f}$ respectively. The first term, f, allows evaluating the local matching of pixels by attributing a label l to each node in a graph $\mathcal{G}$. The second term, $\hat{f}$, allows evaluating the smoothness constraint by measuring how well label l fits pixel p given the observed data. Some works Felzenszwalb & Huttenlocher (2006) Boykov et al. (2001) consider the smoothness term as the amount of difference between the disparity of neighboring pixels. This can be seen as the cost of assigning a label l' to a node during the inference step, where $\mathcal{L}$ is the set of all the possible disparity values for a given pixel. The Global Energy Minimization function can be formulated as follows (Equation. 15):

$$E(\mathcal{G}) = E_{l \in \mathcal{L}}(f) + E_{l' \in \mathcal{L}}(\hat{f}) \tag{15}$$

The minimization of this energy is performed iteratively by passing messages between all the neighboring nodes. These messages are updated at each iteration, until convergence. However, a node can be represented as a pixel having a vector of parameters such as, typically, its possible labels (i.e. disparities). However, reducing the complexity of the inference algorithm leads in most cases to reduced matching quality. Other algorithm variants can be derived from this basic model by introducing additional parameters in the message to be passed. One of the important parameters is the spatio-colorimetric proximity between nodes Trinh (2008).

– The data term we propose can be defined as a local evaluation of attributing a label l to a node. It is given by Equation 16:

$$E_{l \in \mathcal{L}}(f) = \sum_{p} \alpha \, \phi^{x \to x',y}(z_1) \tag{16}$$

Where $\phi^{x \to x',y}(z_m)$ is the mth dissimilarity cost obtained for each matched pixel $(p^{x',y}, p^{x,y})$. Parameter α is a fuzzy value within the [0,1] interval. It allows to compute a confidence measure for attributing a disparity value d to the pixel p. α is given by Equation 17:

$$\alpha = \begin{cases} \psi(p^{x \to x',y}) & \text{if } \psi(p^{x \to x',y}) \geqslant \varrho \\ 0 & \text{otherwise} \end{cases} \tag{17}$$

Where $\psi(p^{x \to x',y})$ is a confidence measure computed for each pair $(p^{x,y}, p^{x',y})$ of matched pixels and ϱ is a confidence threshold. The way of computing the confidence measures.

– The smoothness term is used to ensure that neighboring pixels have similar disparities.

The two-frame stereo matching approaches allow computing disparities and detecting occlusions, assuming that each pixel in the input image corresponds to a unique depth value. The stereo algorithm described in this section stems from the inference principle based on hierarchical belief propagation and energy minimization.

It takes into account the advantages of local methods for reducing the complexity of the Belief Propagation method which leads to an improvement in the quality of results. A Hierarchical Belief Propagation (HBP) based on a Confidence Measure technique is proposed: first, the data term (detailed in Section 4.1) is computed using the WACD dissimilarity function. The obtained disparity volume allows initializing the Belief Propagation graph by attributing a set of possible labels (i.e. disparities) for each node (i.e. pixels). The originality is to consider a subset of nodes among all the nodes to begin the inference algorithm. This subset is obtained thanks to a confidence measure computed at each node of a graph of connected pixels. Second, the propagation of messages between nodes is performed hierarchically from the nodes having the highest confidence measure to those having the lowest one. A message is a vector of parameters (e.g. possible disparities, (x, y) coordinates, etc.) that describes the state of a node. To begin with, the propagation is performed inside an homogeneous color region and then passed from a region to another. The set of regions are obtained by a color-based segmentation using the MeanShift method Comaniciu & Meer (2002). A summary of our algorithm is given in Algorithm 2:

Algorithm 2 Hierarchical Belief Propagation.

1) Initialize the data cost for nodes in the graph using the method in Fakhfakh et al. (2010).
2) Compute a Confidence Measure $\psi(p^{x \rightarrow x',y})$ for each node.
3) Repeat steps a, b, c and d for each node
  a) Select node (i.e. pixel) $Node_i$, i being the node number, having a data term lower than a confidence threshold ϱ.
  b) Select the k-nearest neighbor nodes within a cubic 3D support window that have a $\psi(p^{x \rightarrow x',y})$ greater than ϱ.
  c) Update the label of the current node.
  d) Update the weight of the current node.
4) Repeat step 3) until reaching minimal energy.

4.2 Selective matching approach

Using the WACD dissimilarity function allows initializing the set of labels. It represents a first estimate of the disparity map which contains matching errors. Then, each pair of pixels is evaluated using the Confidence Measure method described in Fakhfakh et al. (2009). The likelihood function used to initialize the disparity set is applied to each pixel of the image. Furthermore, for each matched pair of pixels a confidence measure is computed. It is termed $\psi(p_l^{x,y}, p_r^{x',y})$ which represents the level of certainty of considering a label l as the best label for pixel p. This confidence measure function depends on several local parameters and is given by Equation 18:

$$\psi(p_l^{x,y}, p_r^{x',y}) = P(p_r^{x',y} / p_l^{x,y}, \rho, min, \sigma, \omega) \tag{18}$$

The confidence measure with its parameters is given by Equation 19:

$$\psi(p_l^{x,y}, p_r^{x,y'}) = \left(1 - \frac{min}{\omega}\right)^{\tau^2 log(\sigma)} \tag{19}$$

Where

– *Best Correlation Score (min):* The output of the dissimilarity function is a measure of the degree of similarity between two pixels. Then, the candidate pixels are ranked in increasing order according to their corresponding scores. The couple of pixels that has the minimum score is considered as the best-matched pixels. The lower the score, the better the matching.

The nearer the minimum score to zero, the greater the chance of the candidate pixel to be the actual correspondent.

– *Number of Potential Candidate Pixels (τ):* This parameter represents the number of potential candidate pixels having similar scores. τ has a big influence because it reflects the behavior of the dissimilarity function. A high value of τ means that the first candidate pixel is located in a uniform color region of the frame. The lower the value of τ, the fewer the candidate pixels. If there are few candidates, the chosen candidate pixel has a greater chance of being the actual correspondent. Indeed, the pixel to be matched belongs to a region with high variation of color components. A very small value of τ and a min score close to zero, means that the pixel to be matched probably belongs to a region of high color variation.

– *Disparity variation of the τ pixels (σ):* A disparity value is obtained for each candidate pixel. For the τ potential candidate pixels, we compute the standard deviation σ of the τ disparity values. A small σ means that the τ candidate pixels are spatially neighbors. In this case, the true candidate pixel should belong to a particular region of the frame, such as an edge or a transition point. Therefore, it increases the confidence measure. A large σ means that the τ candidate pixels taken into account are situated in a uniform color region.

– *Gap value (ω):* This parameter represents the difference between the τth and $(\tau+1)^{th}$ scores given with the dissimilarity function used. It is introduced to adjust the impact of the minimum score.

To ensure that function ψ has a value between 0 and 1, a few constraints are introduced. The min parameter must not be higher than ω. If so, parameter ω is forced to $min + 1$. Moreover, the $log(\sigma)$ term is used instead of σ, so as to reduce the impact of high value of σ and obtain coherent confidence measures. The number τ of potential candidate pixels is deduced from the $\mathcal{L}$ scores obtained with the WACD likelihood function. The main idea is to detect major differences between successive scores. These major differences are called main gaps. Let ϕ denote a discrete function which represents all the scores given by the dissimilarity function in increasing order. We introduced a second function denoted η, which represents the average growth rate of the ϕ function. η can be seen as the ratio of the difference between a given score and the first score, and the difference between their ranks. This function is defined in Equation 20:

$$\eta(\phi^{x',y}) = \frac{\phi^{x',y}(z_m) - \phi^{x',y}(z_1)}{z_m - z_1} \qquad m \in \mathcal{L} \tag{20}$$

where $\phi^{x',y}(z_m)$ is the mth dissimilarity cost among the $\mathcal{L}$ scores obtained for the pair of matched pixels $(p^{x,y}, p^{x',y})$. z_m is the rank of the mth score. $\eta(\phi^{x',y})$ is a discrete function that allows to highlight the large gaps between scores. It is materialized using Equation 21:

$$\xi(\phi^{x',y}) = \begin{cases} \frac{\nabla\eta^{x',y}}{m^2} & \text{if } \nabla\eta^{x',y} \geqslant 0 \\ -1 & \text{otherwise} \end{cases} \tag{21}$$

The previous function (Equation 7) is used to characterize the major scores and is applied only in the case where the gradient $\nabla\eta^{x',y}$ has a positive sign. We have introduced parameter m^2 in order to penalize the candidate pixels according to their rank. The number of candidate pixels is given by Equation 22:

$$\tau = \arg\max_{m} \xi(\phi^{x',y}) \tag{22}$$

4.3 Hierarchical belief propagation

The inference algorithm based on a belief propagation method Felzenszwalb & Huttenlocher (2006) can be applied to reach the optimal solution that corresponds to the best disparity set. A set of messages are iteratively transmitted from a node to its neighbors until convergence. This global optimization is NP-hard and far from real time. Referring to this basic framework, all the nodes have the same weight. The main drawback is that several erroneous messages might be passed across the graph, leading moreover to an increase in the number of iterations without guarantee of reaching the best solution. Several works have tried to decrease the number of iterations of the belief propagation method. The proposed HBP technique allows an improvement in both quality of results and processing time compared with the state of the art. The main ideas of the HBP are as follows:

– The confidence measure is used to assign a weight to each node in the graph. At each iteration, messages are passed hierarchically from nodes having a high confidence measure (i.e. high weight) to nodes having a low confidence measure (i.e. small weight). A high weight means a high certainty of the message to be passed. The weights of the nodes are updated after each iteration, so that a subset of nodes is activated to be able to send messages in the next iteration.

– The propagation is first performed inside a consistent color region, and then passed to the neighboring regions. The set of regions is obtained by a color-based segmentation using the MeanShift method Comaniciu & Meer (2002).

– In our framework, the messages are passed differently from the standard BP algorithm. Instead of considering the 4-connected nodes, the k-nearest neighboring nodes are considered. These k-nearest neighboring nodes belong to a 3D support window. We assume that the labels of nodes vary smoothly within a 3D support window centered on the node to be updated.

5. Experimental results

5.1 Evaluation of the obstacle extraction module

The first proposed module is evaluated on real-world data in outdoor environments in various weather conditions. The datasets concern videosurveillance system in which a stationary camera monitors real-worlds, such as a level crossing. The four datasets include: "Pontet" and "Chamberonne", which are two level crossings in Switzerland in cloudy weather, given that test images were 384 × 288 pixels; a dataset entitled "Pan", which represents a level crossing in France in sunny weather, given that test images were 720 × 576; and a dataset taken in snowy weather in EPFL–Switzerland is also considered for the evaluation. The test images are the same size as the "Pontet" and "Chamberonne" datasets. For a qualitative evaluation purpose, 1000 of foreground ground truths images have been obtained by manual segmentation from the "Pontet" and "Chamberonne" datasets. This allows computing the recall and the precision of the detection. In the experiments, the proposed framework is compared with the Mixture Of Gaussians (MOG) and Codebook algorithms. Furthermore, ICA model is evaluated on different color spaces and different color constancy. The obtained results are also compared with those obtained from gray scale images. The algorithms are implemented in Visual Studio C++ 2008, using the OpenCV and IT++ libraries. The four datasets are given in Figure 5.

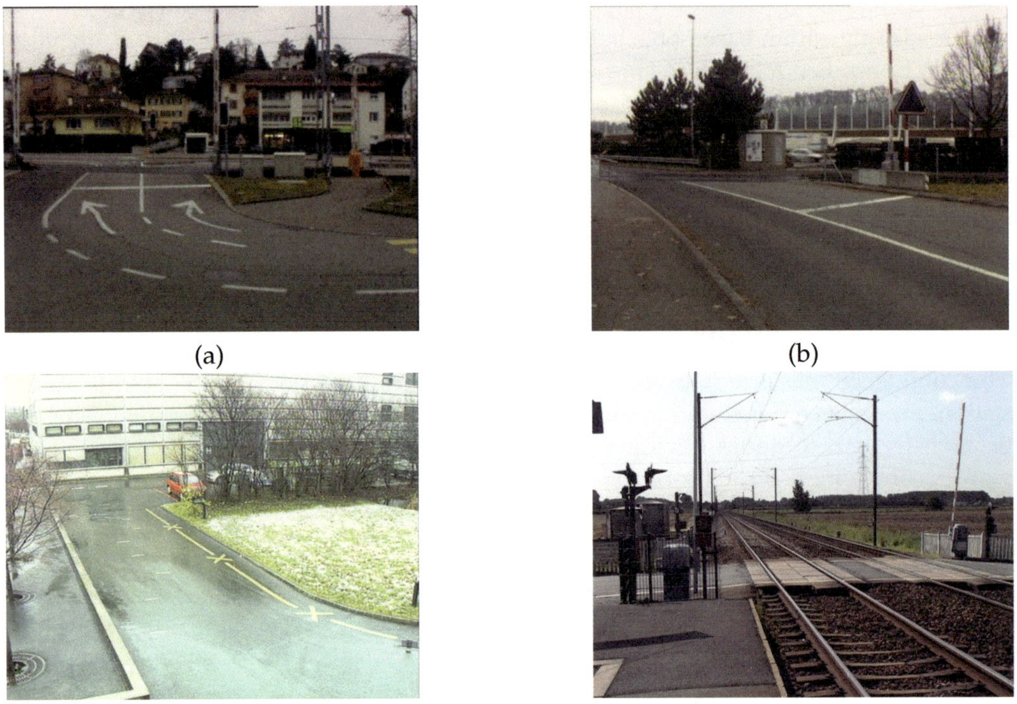

(a) (b) (c) (d)

Fig. 5. The four datasets used for the evaluation (a) pontet: a level crossing in Lausanne–Switzerland (b) chamberonne: a level crossing in Lausanne–Switzerland (c) EPFL–Parking (d) pan: a level crossing in France.

5.1.1 Quantitative evaluation

The performance of the proposed scheme is compared to the two best-known techniques, which are the pixel-wise Gaussian Mixture Model (GMM) and Codebook. These algorithms are chosen because of their algorithmic complexity, which is close to ours. This qualitative comparison is performed by comparing the segmentation results of each algorithm with a ground truth. The ground truth is established by a manual segmentation of moving and stationary foreground objects in the image sequence. The evaluation criterion is expressed by the *Recall* and *Precision* parameters which describe the way the segmented image matches the corresponding ground truth. The *Recall* measures the ability of an algorithm to detect the true foreground pixels, while the *Precision* is an intrinsic criterion which gives a clue to the accuracy of the detection. These parameters can be expressed in terms of true positives T_p, true negatives T_n, false positives F_p and false negatives F_n terms. The *Recall* and *Precision* are obtained by Equation 23 and 24:

$$Recall = \frac{T_p}{T_p + F_n} \tag{23}$$

$$Precision = \frac{T_p}{T_p + F_p} \tag{24}$$

where T_p represents the number of well pixels classified as foreground, compared to the ground truth, F_n is the number of pixels classified as background, whereas they are really foreground pixels while referring to the ground truth, and F_p is the number of pixels classified as foreground, whereas they are really background pixels. $T_p + F_n$ can be seen as the number of the true foreground pixels obtained by the ground truth, while $T_p + F_p$ is the foreground pixels classified by a given algorithm. The image samples used for computing these two previous parameters are taken from the two datasets *Pontet* and *Chamberonne*, given that five hundred images from the each dataset are used for a manual extraction of foreground objects. This allows obtaining a ground truth dataset from which the different algorithms are evaluated. Table 1 shows the qualitative evaluation of the foreground extraction process, given by *Recall* and *Precision* measures:

	MOG	**Codebook**	**ACI+Filtering**
Recall	94.76%	93.49%	96.14%
Precision	95.87%	91.72%	97.34%

Table 1. Qualitative evaluation given by *Recall* and *Precision* measures.

A visual comparison of our method compared with two other methods from the literature is given by fugure 6.

The implementation of the proposed framework runs on a personal computer with an Intel 32-bit 3.1-GHz processor. For the Pontet dataset, the proposed algorithm runs at a speed of 13 fps (frame per second). The processing time of our algorithm is compared with MOG and Codebook algorithms. Table 2 shows that our algorithm is faster than the other algorithms.

Algorithms	Proposed algorithm	MOG	Codebook
Processing time	88.687 *ms*	286.588 *ms*	118.402 *ms*

Table 2. Processing time of Pontet dataset.

5.2 Evaluation of the 3D localization module

The proposed depth estimation for 3D localization algorithm is first evaluated on the Middlebury stereo benchmark (`http://www.middlebury.edu/stereo`), using the Tsukuba, Venus, Teddy and Cones standard datasets. The evaluation concerns non occluded regions (nonocc), all regions (all) and depth-discontinuity regions (disc). In the first step of our algorithm, the WACD likelihood function is first performed on all the pixels. Applying the *winner-take-all* strategy, a label corresponding to the best estimated disparity is attributed to each pixel. The second step consists in selecting a subset of pixels according to their confidence

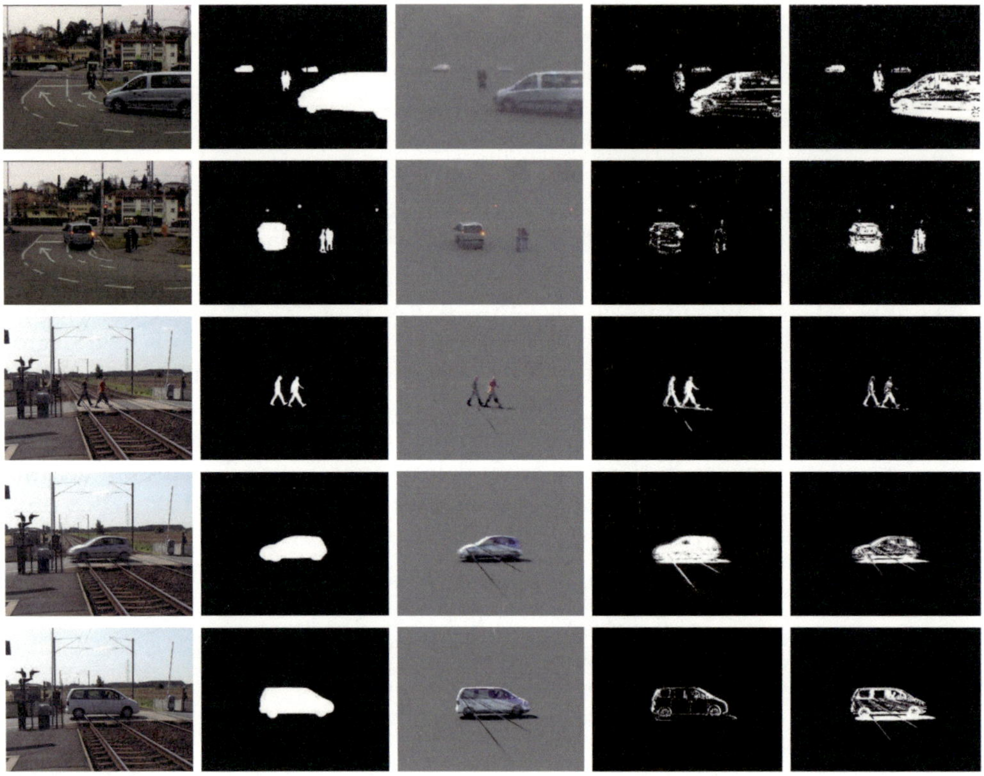

(a) (b) (c) (d) (e)

Fig. 6. Visual comparison of our algorithm with other methods. (a) original images (b) ground truth (c) changes detection obtained with our method (d) with MOG method and (e) with Codebook method.

measure. Indeed, the pixels having a low confidence measure belongs to either occluded or textureless regions. However, the subset corresponding to the well-matched pixels is taken as the starting point of the hierarchical belief propagation module.

Quantitatively, our method was compared to several other methods from the literature. These methods are H-Cut Miyazaki et al. (2009), max-product Felzenszwalb & Huttenlocher (2006) and PhaseBased El-Etriby et al. (2007). Table 3 provides quantitative comparison results between all four methods. This table shows the percentage of pixels incorrectly matched for the non-occluded pixels (nonocc), the discontinuity pixels (disc), and for all the matched pixels (all). More specifically, the proposed method is better for Tsukuba in "all" and "disc" pixels, in Venus for "disc" pixels and in Cones for "all" pixels.

Figure 7 illustrates an example of two objects extracted from the Cones and Teddy images, respectively. The face extracted from Cones corresponds to an non-occluded region while the teddy bear corresponds to a depth discontinuity. This proves that the propagation of disparities preserves the discontinuity between regions and gives a good accuracy in terms of matching pixels in the non-occluded regions.

Algorithm	*Tsukuba*			*Venus*			*Teddy*			*Cones*		
	nonocc	*all*	*disc*	*nonocc*	*all*	*disc*	*nonocc*	*all*	*disc*	*nonocc*	*all*	*disc*
H-Cut	2.85	4.86	14.4	1.73	3.14	20.2	10.7	19.5	25.8	5.46	15.6	15.7
Proposed	**4.87**	**5.04**	**8.47**	**3.42**	**3.99**	**10.5**	**17.5**	**20.8**	**28.0**	**7.46**	**12.5**	**13.3**
Max-Product	1.88	3.78	10.1	1.31	2.34	15.7	24.6	32.4	34.7	21.2	28.5	30.1
PhaseBased	4.26	6.53	15.4	6.71	8.16	26.4	14.5	23.1	25.5	10.8	20.5	21.2

Table 3. Algorithm evaluation on the Middlebury dataset

(a) (b) (c) (d) (e) (f)

Fig. 7. Different steps of our algorithm in different types of regions. (a) Left image (b) Segmented face and teddy bear extracted from the Cones and Teddy images, respectively, using Mean Shift (c) Dense disparity map obtained using WACD (d) Sparse disparity map corresponding to the well-matched pixels, with 60% confidence threshold (e) Dense disparity map after performing the HBP (f) Corresponding ground truth.

The disparity allows estimating the 3-D position and spatial occupancy rate of each segmented object. The transformation of an image plane point $p = \{x, y\}$ into a 3-D reference system point $P = \{X, Y, Z\}$ must be performed. The distance of an object point is calculated by triangulation, assuming parallel optical axes:

$$Z = \frac{b.f}{d} \tag{25}$$

Where
– Z is the depth, i.e. the distance between the sensor camera and the object point along the Z axis,
– f is the focal length, i.e. the distance between the lens and the sensor, supposed identical for both cameras,

– b is the baseline, i.e. the distance separating the cameras.
– d is the estimated disparity.

The proposed 3D localization algorithm is evaluated on image sequences of long of one hour acquired on two real level crossings. We have used a system composed of two cameras of model Sony DXC-390/390P 3-CCD with an optical lens of model Cinegon 3 CCD Lens 5.3mm FL. The cameras are fixed on a metal support of 1.5 meter of height, and the distance between their optical axis is fixed at 0.4 meter. The whole is placed at around 20 meters far from the dangerous zone. We illustrate in figure 8 an example of two pedestrians extracted by the stICA algorithm from the left-hand image. The image (b) is estimated by applying the WACD local stereo matching algorithm allows us to obtain a first disparity map which contains a lot of errors of matching. Much of them are identified by applying the confidence measure function. Only the pairs of matched pixels having a confidence measure higher than 60% as threshold, are kept (image c). These retained pixels are considered as a starting point for the belief propagation algorithm leading to estimate the disparity of the remaining pixels (image d). This example show the accuracy of the 3D localization in a case of occlusion, knowing that the two pedestrians are at two different distances from the cameras.

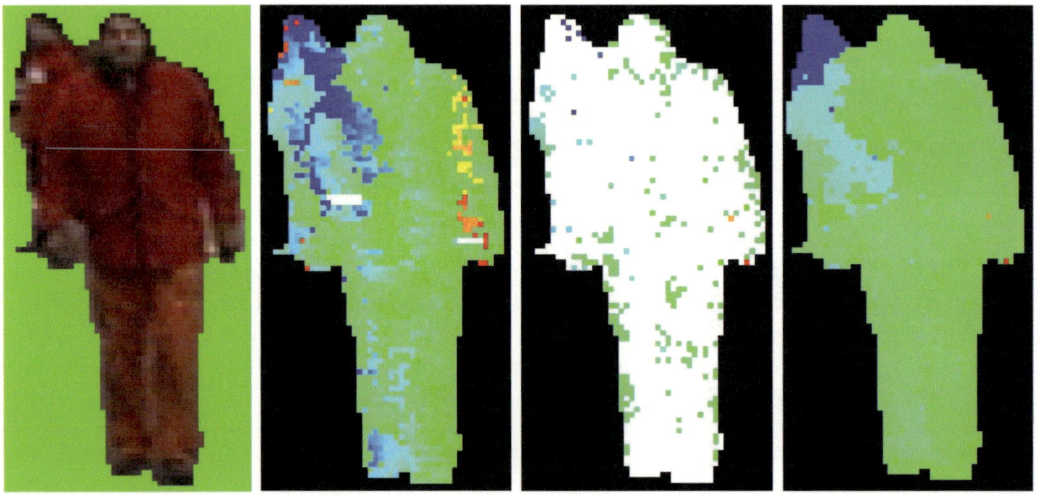

(a) (b) (c) (d)

Fig. 8. 3D localization of two pedestrians partially occluded. (a) pedestrians extracted by stICA, (b) first disparity map obtained with the WACD algorithm, (c) sparse disparity map obtained after applying the confidence measure function, (d) final disparity map obtained with the selective belief propagation algorithm.

We illustrate in figure 9 some examples of obstacles which are extracted and localized with the proposed algorithms (from (a) to (d)). The first column corresponds to the left-hand images acuiqres from the left camera. The middle column represents the first disparity map obtained from the WACD stereo matching algorithm. Hence, the last column correspond to the final disparity map which will allows localizing all of obstacles in the 3D space.

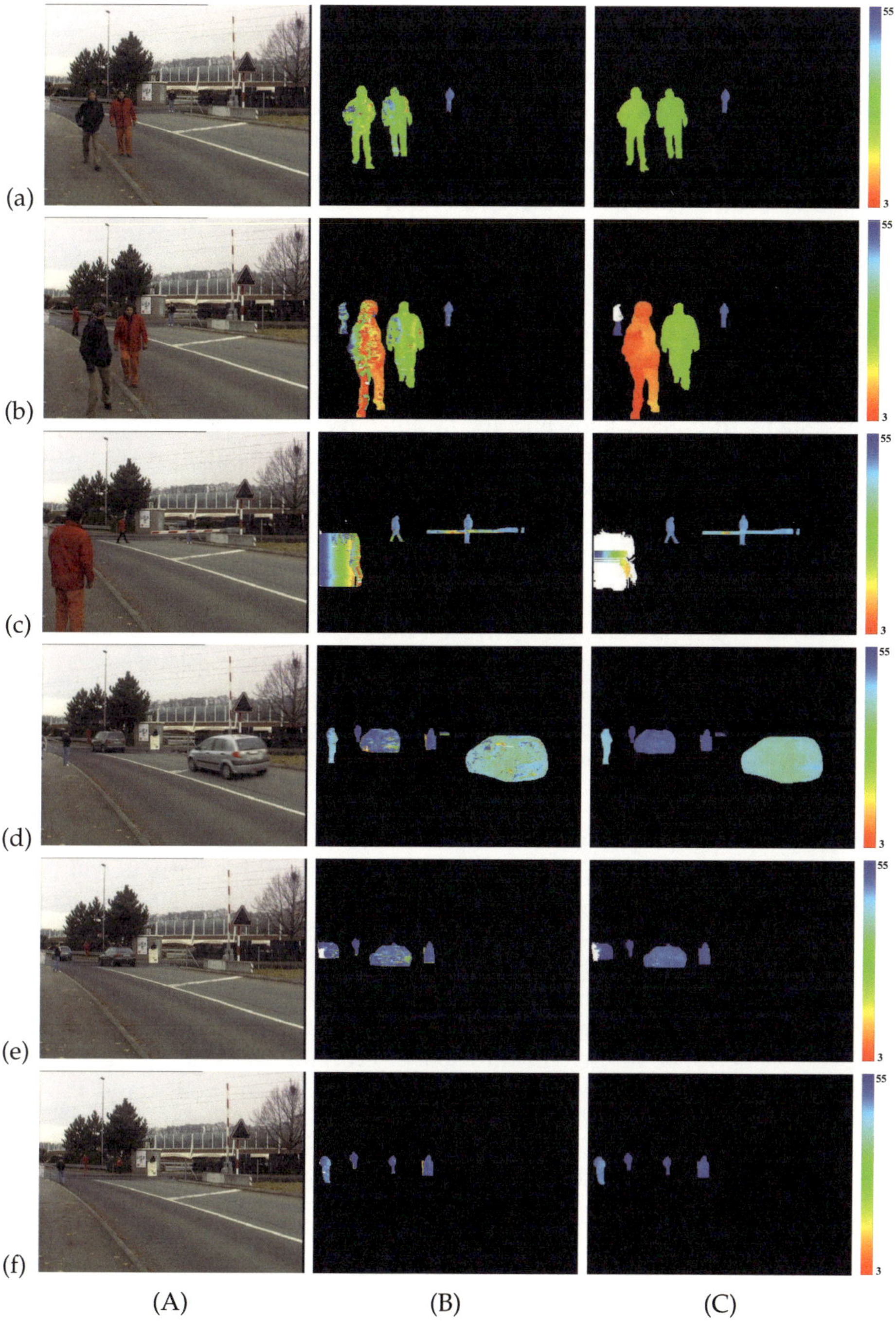

Fig. 9. 3D localization steps of a given scenario. (A) left-hand image, (B) dense disparity map obtained by applying WACD correlation function, (C) final disparity map obtained after applying the Selective Belief Propagation.

6. Conclusion

In this chapter we have proposed a processing chain addressing safety at level crossings composed of two steps : a background subtraction based on Spatio-temporal Idependentent Component Analysis and a robust 3D localization by global stereo matching algorithm. It is to be noted that the 3D localization is only applied on stationary and moving obstacles. The foreground extraction method based on stICA has already been evaluated in terms of Recall (95%) and Precision (98%), on a set of 1000 images with manually elaborated ground truth. Real-world datasets have been shot at three different level crossings and a parking at the EPFL institute including a hundred scenarios per level crossing under different illumination and weather conditions. This first step is compared with two well-known robust algorithms, entitled GMM and Codebook, from which it proves it effectiveness in term of precision of foreground extraction and processing time. The stereo matching algorithm is first applied on a standard dataset known as the Middlebury Setreo Vision which represents an unique framework for comparison with the state-of-the-art. The latter proves it effectiveness compared to stereo matching algorithms found in the literature.

The experimentations showed that the method is applicable to real-world scenes in level crossing applications. The main output of the proposed system is an accurate 3D localization of any object in, and around a level crossing. According to the experimentations, the localization of some objects may fail. However, the localization of one among sixty objects fails, this is due to the smaller number of pixels having confidence measure larger than a fixed threshold or the occlusion problem. The starting point of the belief propagation process highly depends on the number and repartition of pixels, having hight confidence measure, inside an object. This drawback can be handled by introducing the temporal dependency in the belief propagation process.

For safety purposes, the proposed system will be coupled with already existing devices at level crossings. For instance, the status of the traffic light and the barriers will be taken as input in our vision-based system. The level of such an alarm depends on the configuration of the different parameters. For instance, the presence of an obstacle in the crossing zone when the barriers are lowering is a dangerous situation and the triggered alarm must be of high importance. A Preliminary Risk Analysis (PRA) seems to be an interesting way to categorize the level of alarms. In the frame of the French project entitled PANSafer, these different parameters will be studied. In particular, telecommunication systems will be used to inform road users on the status of the level crossing. Such informations could also be shared with train driver and control room. The communication tool and the nature of information to be transmitted are in study.

7. References

Boykov, Y., Veksler, O. & Zabih, R. (2001). Fast approximate energy minimization via graph cuts, *IEEE Transactions on PAMI* 23(11): 1222–1239.

Cardoso, J.-F. (1997). Adaptive blind separation of independent sources: a deflation approach, *IEEE Letters on Signal Processing*, Vol. 4, pp. 112–114.

Comaniciu, D. & Meer, P. (2002). Mean shift: A robust approach toward feature space analysis, *IEEE Transactions on Pattern Analysis and Machine Intelligence (PAMI)* 24(5): 603–619.

Cvejic, N., Bull, D. & Canagarajah, N. (2007). Improving fusion of surveilliance images in sensor networks using independent component analysis, *IEEE Trans. On Consumer Electronics* 53(3): 1029–1035.

Delfosse, N. & Loubaton, P. (1995). Infomax and maximum likelihood for sources separation, *IEEE Letters on Signal Processing*, Vol. 45, pp. 59–83.

Dun, B. V., Wouters, J. & Moonen, M. (2007). Improving auditory steady-state response detection using independent component analysis on multichannel eeg data, *IEEE Trans. On Biomedical Engineering* 54(7): 1220–1230.

El-Etriby, S., Al-Hamadi, A. & b. Michaelis (2007). Desnse stereo correspondance with slanted surface using phase-based algorithm, *In : IEEE International Symposium on Indistrual Electronic*.

Elgammal, A., Harwood, D. & Davis, L. (2000). Non-parametric model for background subtraction, *ECCV*.

Fakhfakh, N., Khoudour, L., El-Koursi, E., Bruyelle, J.-L., Dufaux, A., & Jacot, J. (2011). 3d objects localization using fuzzy approach and hierarchical belief propagation : application at level crossings, *In EURASIP Journal on Image and Video Processing* 2011(4): 1–15.

Fakhfakh, N., Khoudour, L., El-Koursi, E., Jacot, J. & Dufaux, A. (2010). A video-based object detection system for improving safety at level crossings, *In Open Transportation Journal* 5: 1–15.

Fakhfakh, N., Khoudour, L., El-Koursi, M., Jacot, J. & Dufaux, A. (2009). A new selective confidence measure-based approach for stereo matching, *International Conference on Knowledge-Based and Intelligent Information and Engineering Systems, Springer-Verlag Berlin Heidelberg*, Vol. 5711, Santiago, Chile, pp. 184–191.

Felzenszwalb, P. & Huttenlocher, D. (2006). Efficient belief propagation for early vision, *International Journal of Computer Vision (IJCV)* 70(1): 41–54.

Foggia, P., Jolion, J., Limongiello, A. & Vento, M. (2007). Stereo vision for obstacle detection: A graph-based approach, *Lecture Notes in Computer Science, Springer Berlin / Heidelberg*, pp. 37–48.

Foresti, G. (1998). A real-time system for video surveillance of unattended outdoor environments, *IEEE Transactions on Circuits and Systems for Video Technology* 8(6): 697–704.

Griffioen, E. (2004). Improving level crossings using findings from human behaviour studies, *Proc. of 8th Inter. Level Crossing Symposium*.

Kim, K., Chalidabhongse, T., Harwood, D. & Davis, L. (2005). Real-time foregroundŰbackground segmentation using codebook model, *Journal of Real-Time Imaging, Special Issue on Video Object Processing* 11(3): 172–185.

Lee, C. & Ho, Y. (2008). Disparity estimation using belief propagation for view interpolation, *In: ITC-CSC*, Japan, pp. 21–24.

McKeown, M., Makeig, S., Brown, G., Jung, T., ndermann, S., Bell, A. & Sejnowski, T. (1998). Analysis of fmri data by blind separation into independent spatial components, *Human Brain Mappin* 6(3): 160–188.

Miyazaki, D., Matsushita, Y. & Ikeuchi, K. (2009). Interactive shadow removal from a single image using hierarchical graph cut, *In : Asian Conference on Computer Vision (ACCV)*.

Nelson, A. (2002). The uk approach to managing risk at passive level crossings, *Inter. Symposium on RailRoad-Highway Grade Crossing Research and Safety, 7th*.

Ohta, M. (2005). Level crossings obstacle detection system using stereo cameras, *Quarterly Report of RTRI* 46(2): 110–117.

Oja, E., Ogawa, H. & Wangviwattana, J. (1991). Learning in nonlinear constrained hebbian networks, *T.Kohonen, et al .,editor, Artificial Neural Networks,Proc.ICANN*, Espoo, Finland, Amsterdam, Holland, pp. 385–390.

Stauffer, C. & Grimson, W. (2000). Learning patterns of activity using real-time tracking, *IEEE Trans. Pattern Anal. Mach. Intell.* 22(8): 747–757.

Taguchi, Y., Wilburn, B. & Zitnick, C. L. (2008). Stereo reconstruction with mixed pixels using adaptive over-segmentation, *CVPR*, Anchorage, Alaska, pp. 1–8.

Trinh, H. (2008). Efficient stereo algorithm using multiscale belief propagation on segmented images, *Proceedings of the Brith Machine Vision Conference (BMVC)*.

Tsai, D. & Lai, S. (2009). Independent component analysis-based background subtraction for indoor surveillance, *IEEE Trans. On Image Processing* 18(1): 158–167.

Waldert, S. (2007). Real-time fetal heart monitoring in biomagnetic measurements using aadaptive real-time ica, *IEEE Trans. On Biomedical Engineering* 54(107): 1964–1874.

Wu, F. (1982). The potts model, *Reviews of Modern Physics* 54(1): 235–268.

Yang, Q., Wang, L., Yang, R., Stewenius, H. & Niste, D. (2009). Stereo matching with color-weighted correlation, hierachical belief propagation, *IEEE Trans. on PAMI* 31(3): 492–504.

Yoda, I., Sakaue, K. & Hosotani, D. (2006). Multi-point stereo camera system for controlling safety at railroad crossings, *IEEE ICVS*.

Zhang, X. & Chen, Z. (2006). An automated video object extraction system based on spatiotemporal independent component analysis and multiscale segmentation, *EURASIP Journal on Applied Signal Processing* 2006(2): 1–22.

Zhen, T. & Zhenjiang, M. (2008). Fast background subtraction using improved gmm and graph cut, *Congress on Image and Signal Processing, CISP*, Vol. 4, Sanya, China, pp. 181–185.

6

Behavior Recognition Using any Feature Space Representation of Motion Trajectories

Shehzad Khalid
Bahria University
Pakistan

1. Introduction

In recent years, there has been a growth of research activity aimed at the development of sophisticated content-based video data management techniques. This development is now especially timely given an increasing number of systems that are able to capture and store data about object motion such as those of humans and vehicles. This has acted as a spur to the development of content-based visual data management techniques for tasks such as behavior classification and recognition, detection of anomalous behavior and object motion prediction. Behavior can obviously be categorized at different levels of granularity. In far-field surveillance, we are primarily interested in trajectory-based coarse motion description involving movement direction (right/left or up/down) and motion type (walking, running or stopping). These techniques are essential for the development of next generation 'actionable intelligence' surveillance systems.

Processing of trajectory data for activity classification and recognition has gained significant interest quite recently. Various techniques have been proposed for modeling of trajectory-based motion activity patterns and using the modeled patterns for classification and anomaly detection. Much of the earlier research focus in motion analysis has been on high-level object trajectory representation schemes that are able to produce compressed forms of motion data (Aghbari et al., 2003; Chang et al., 1998; Dagtas et al., 2000; Hsu & Teng, 2002; Jin & Mokhtarian, 2004; Khalid & Naftel, 2005; Shim & Chang, 2004). This work presupposes the existence of some low-level visual tracking scheme for reliably extracting object-based trajectories (Hu, Tan, Wang & Maybank, 2004; Vlachos et al., 2002). The literature on trajectory-based motion understanding and pattern discovery is less mature but advances using Learning Vector Quantization (LVQ) (Johnson & Hogg, 1995), Self-Organising Maps (SOMs) (Hu, Xiao, Xie, Tan & Maybank, 2004; Owens & Hunter, 2000), Hidden Markov Models (HMMs) (Bashir et al., 2006; 2005b), and fuzzy neural networks (Hu, Xie, Tan & Maybank, 2004) have all been reported. These approaches are broadly categorized into statistical and neural network based approaches.

In a development of trajectory-based motion event recognition systems, there are different questions that we need to answer before proposing or selecting a pattern modeling and recognition technique. These includes:

1. What is the feature space representation of trajectories?

2. What is the distribution of trajectories in a given feature space representation? Do we need to cater for complex shape distributions that may exit in a given motion pattern?
3. Do we expect to have a multimodal distribution of trajectories within a given pattern?

Most of the trajectory-based motion recognition system, as proposed in relevant literature (Hu, Xiao, Xie, Tan & Maybank, 2004; Hu, Xie, Tan & Maybank, 2004; Khalid & Naftel, 2005; 2006; Owens & Hunter, 2000) can operate only on feature space representation of trajectories that lies in Euclidean space with a computable mean. However, a survey of recent literature in the areas of motion feature computation for trajectory representation shows that most of the feature space representation are complex and do not lie in the Euclidean space (Bashir et al., 2006; 2005a;b; 2007; Hamid et al., 2005; Keogh et al., 2001; Xiang & Gong, 2006; Zhong et al., 2004). It is not possible to compute a mean representation of different trajectories using such complex feature spaces. They can therefore not be applied to complex feature spaces with incalculable mean. These approaches expect that the trajectories in a given motion pattern follow certain standard distribution such as Gaussian. They can not cater for multimodal complex shape distribution of trajectories within a given motion pattern which is expected in the presence of complex feature space representation of trajectories. The research presented in this chapter focuses on presenting a trajectory-based behavior recognition and anomaly detection system that have an answer to all of the above raised questions. The proposed approach does not impose any limitation on the representation of trajectories. It can operate using any trajectory representation in any feature space with a given distance function. The proposed approach can perform modeling, classification and anomaly detection in the presence of multimodal distribution of trajectories within a given motion pattern.

The remainder of the chapter is organized as follows: We review some relevant background material in section 2. In section 3, we present a framework of multimodal modeling of activity patterns using any feature space with a computable similarity function. A soft classification and anomaly detection techniques using multimodal m-Medoids model is presented in section 4. Comparative evaluation of currently proposed multimodal m-Medoids and previously proposed localized m-Medoids (Khalid, 2010a) based appraoch for activity classification and anomaly detection is presented in section 5. Experiments have been performed to show the effectiveness of proposed system for trajectory-based modeling, classification and anomaly detection in the presence of multimodal distribution of trajectories within a pattern, as compared to competitors. These experiments are reported in section 6. The last section summarizes the paper.

2. Background and related work

Motion trajectory descriptors are known to be useful candidates for video indexing and retrieval schemes. Variety of trajectory modeling techniques have been proposed to compute the feature for trajectory representation. Most of the techniques for learning motion behaviour patterns and recognition from trajectories use discrete point sequence vectors as input to a machine learning algorithm. Related work within the data mining community on representation schemes for indexing time series data is also relevant to the parameterisation of object trajectories. An object trajectory can be defined as a set of points representing the ordered observations of the location of a moving object made at different points in time. A trajectory can therefore be represented as a time series implying that indexing techniques for time series are also applicable to motion data. For example, Discrete Fourier Transforms (DFT) (Faloutsos et al., 1994), Discrete Wavelet Transforms (DWT) (Chan & Fu, 1999), Adaptive Piecewise Constant Approximations (APCA) (Keogh et al., 2001), and Chebyshev polynomials (Cai & Ng, 2004) have been used to conduct similarity search in time series data. Previous work has also sought to represent moving object trajectories through piecewise linear or quadratic interpolation functions (Chang et al., 1998; Jeanin & Divakaran, 2001), motion histograms (Aghbari et al., 2003) or discretised direction-based schemes (Dagtas et al., 2000; Shim & Chang, 2001; 2004). Spatiotemporal representations using piecewise-defined polynomials were proposed by (Hsu & Teng, 2002), although consistency in applying a trajectory-splitting scheme across query and searched trajectories can be problematic. Affine and more general spatiotemporally invariant schemes for trajectory retrieval have also been presented (Bashir et al., 2003; 2004; Jin & Mokhtarian, 2004). The importance of selecting the most appropriate trajectory model and similarity search metric has received relatively scant attention (Khalid & Naftel, 2005).

Modeling of motion patterns using trajectory data to perform motion based behavior recognition and anomaly detection has gained significant interest recently. Various techniques have been proposed for modeling of motion activity patterns and using the modeled patterns for classification and anomaly detection. These approaches are broadly categorized into statistical and neural network based approaches. Almost all statistical approaches dealing with anomaly detection are based on modelling the density of training data and rejecting test patterns that fall in regions of low density. There are various approaches that use Gaussian mixture models to estimate the probability density of data (Brotherton et al., 1998; Roberts & Tarassenko, 1994; Yeung & Chow, 2002). Various techniques based on hidden Markov models (HMM) have also been proposed (Xiang & Gong, 2005; 2006; Zhang et al., 2005). (Yacoob & Black, 1999) and (Bashir et al., 2005b; 2007) have presented a framework for modeling and recognition of human motion based on a trajectory segmentation scheme. A framework is presented to estimate the multimodal probability density function (PDF), based on PCA coefficients of the sub-trajectories, using GMM. Different classes of object motion are modelled by a continuous HMM per class where the state PDFs are represented by GMMs. The proposed technique has been shown to work for sign language recognition. The proposed classification system can not handle anomalies in test data and can only classify samples from normal patterns. (Xiang & Gong, 2005; 2006) propose a framework for behavior classification and anomaly detection in video sequences. Natural grouping of behaviour patterns is learnt through unsupervised model selection and feature selection on the eigenvectors of a normalized affinity matrix. A Multi-Observation Hidden Markov Model is used for modelling the behaviour pattern. (Hu et al., 2006; 2007) and (Khalid & Naftel, 2006) models normal motion patterns by estimating single multimodal gaussian for each class. For anomaly detection in (Hu et al., 2006), the probability of a trajectory belonging to each motion pattern is calculated. If the probability of association of trajectory to the closest motion pattern is less then a threshold, the trajectory is treated as anomalous. In (Rea et al., 2004), a semantic event detection technique based on discrete HMMs is applied to snooker videos. (Zhang et al., 2005) propose a semi-supervised model using HMMs for anomaly detection. Temporal dependencies are modelled using HMMs. The probability density function of each HMM state is assumed to be a GMM. (Owens & Hunter, 2000) uses Self Organizing Feature Maps (SOFM) to learn normal trajectory patterns. While classifying trajectories, if the distance of the trajectory to its allocated class exceeds a threshold value, the trajectory is identified as anomalous.

In our previous work (Khalid, 2010b), we have proposed *m*-Medoids based activity Modeling and Classification approach using low dimensional feature vector representation of trajectories in Euclidean Space (MC-ES). *m*-Medoids based approach models a pattern by a set of cluster centres of mutually disjunctive sub-classes (referred to as medoids) within the pattern. Once the *m*-Medoids model for all the classes have been learnt, the MC-ES approach performs classification of new trajectories and anomaly detection by checking the closeness of said trajectories to the models of different classes using hierarchical classifier. The anomaly detection module required specification of threshold which is used globally for all the patterns. However, this approach had unaddressed issues like manual specification of threshold for anomaly detection, identification of appropriate value of threshold for anomaly detection and anomaly detection of motion patterns with different scale and orientation which is used globally for all the patterns. These issues are addressed by a localized *m*-Medoids based approach (LMC-ES) as proposed in (Khalid, 2010a) which enables us to automatically select a local significance parameter for each pattern taking into consideration the distribution of individual patterns. LMC-ES can effectively handle patterns with different orientation and scale and has been shown to give superior performance than competitors including GMM, HMM and SVM based classifiers. However, there are still open issues (i) Modeling, classification and anomaly detection in the presence of multimodal distribution of trajectories within a pattern (ii) Soft classification in the presence of multimodal pattern distribution to minimize misclassification (iii) Modeling and classification in feature spaces for which we can not compute mean.

The contribution of this work is to present an extension of *m*-Medoids based modeling approach, wherein the multimodal distribution of samples in each pattern is represented using multimodal *m*-Medoids. An approach for multimodal model-based classification and anomaly detection is also presented. The presented mechanism is based on a soft classification approach which enables the proposed multimodal classifier to adapt to the multimodal distribution of samples within different patterns. The multimodal *m*-Medoids based modeling and classification is applicable to any feature spaces with a computable pairwise similarity measure.

3. Multimodal m-Medoids based modeling

Given a representation of trajectories in any feature space for a given motion pattern, we wish to model the underlying distribution of trajectories within a pattern using training data. A pattern is modeled by a set of cluster centers of mutually disjunctive sub-classes (referred to as medoids) within the pattern. The proposed modeling technique referred to as *m*-Medoids modeling, models the class containing *n* members with *m* medoids known *a-priori*. Modeling of pattern using multimodal *m*-Medoids approach in general feature space is a three step process, (i) identification of *m* medoids, (ii) computation of set of possible normality ranges for the pattern and (iii) selection of customized normality range for each medoid. The resulting models of identified patterns can then be used to classify new unseen trajectory data to one of the modeled classes or identify it as anomalous if it is significantly distant from all of the modeled pattern.

3.1 Step 1: Identification of m-Medoids

The algorithm for identification of medoids using finite dimensional features in general feature space with a computable similarity matrix is based on the affinity propagation based clustering algorithm (Frey & Dueck, 2007). Let $DB^{(i)}$ be the classified training samples associated to pattern i, the modeling algorithm comprises the following steps:

1. Form the affinity matrix $A \in R^{n \times n}$ defined by

$$A(a,b) = \begin{cases} exp\left(\frac{-dist(s_a,s_b)}{2\sigma^2}\right) & ifa \neq b \\ P(a) & otherwise \end{cases} \tag{1}$$

   Here $s_a, s_b \in DB^{(i)}$, σ is the scaling parameter and $P(a)$ is the preference parameter indicating the suitability of sample a to be selected as an exemplar (medoid). We set $P(a)$ to the median of affinities of sample a with n samples. We use a dynamic value of σ which is set to be the 6th nearest neighbor of s_a to cater for variation in local distribution of trajectory samples.
2. Initialize availability matrix $\Im(a,b) = 0 \;\; \forall a,b$. The entry $\Im(a,b)$ in availability matrix stores the suitability of trajectory s_b to be selected by trajectory s_a as its exemplar.
3. Update responsibility matrix $\Re$ as

$$\Re(a,b) = A(a,b) - max_{\forall c \text{ s.t. } b \neq c} \{\Im(a,c), A(a,c)\} \tag{2}$$

   The entry $\Re(a,b)$ in the responsibility matrix reflects the accumulated evidence for how well-suited trajectory s_b to serve as an exemplar for trajectory s_a while taking into account other potential exemplar for trajectory s_a.
4. Update availability matrix $\Im$ as

$$\Im(a,b) = \begin{cases} \min\{0, \Re(b,b) + \sum_{\forall c \text{ s.t. } c \neq a \wedge c \neq b}\}\{0, \Re(c,b)\} & ifa \neq b \\ \sum_{\forall c \text{ s.t. } a \neq c} \max\{0, \Re(c,a)\} & otherwise \end{cases} \tag{3}$$

5. Identify the exemplar for each sample as

$$\xi_a = argmax_b[\Im(a,b) + \Re(a,b)] \tag{4}$$

6. Iterate through steps 3-5 till the algorithm is converged or maximum number of learning iterations (t_{max}) is exceeded. The algorithm is considered to have converged if there is no change in exemplar identification for certain number of iterations ($t_{convergance}$).
7. If the number of exemplars identified are smaller than the desired number of medoids, set higher values of preference and vice versa. The algorithm is repeated till the desired number of exemplars are identified. An appropriate value of preference parameter, for identification of desired number of medoids, is searched using a bisection method.
8. Append exemplars ξ_a to the list of medoids $\mathbf{M}^{(i)}$ modeling the pattern i.

3.2 Step 2: Computation of possible normality ranges

After the identification of medoids $\mathbf{M}^{(i)}$ for pattern i, we intend to identify and pre-compute a set of possible normality ranges for a given pattern. Values of normality ranges for a given pattern is determined by the inter-medoid distances within a given pattern. Hence, different patterns will have different set of possible normality ranges depending on the distribution of samples, and in turn medoids, within a pattern. In this step, a set of possible normality ranges $\mathbf{D}^{(c)}$ for the pattern c is computed as follows:

1. Identify the closest pair of medoids (i,j) (indexed by (p,q)) from $\mathbf{M}^{(c)}$ as follows:

$$(p,q) = arg\ min_{(i,j)} dist(M_i, M_j) \qquad \forall i,j \wedge i \neq j \tag{5}$$

   where dist(.,.) is the distance function for a given feature space representation of trajectories.
2. Set $l = 1$.
3. Populate the distance array at index l using

$$\mathbf{D}_l^{(c)} = dist(M_p, M_q) \tag{6}$$

4. Remove the closest pair of medoids using

$$\mathbf{M}^{(c)} = \mathbf{M}^{(c)} - \{M_p, M_q\} \tag{7}$$

5. Set $l = l + 1$.
6. Iterate through steps 1-5 till there are no mediods left in $\mathbf{M}^{(c)}$.

3.3 Step 3: Selection of customized normality range for each medoid

After the identification of medoids and a set of possible normality ranges for a given pattern, we select different normality range for each medoid depending on the distribution of samples from the same and different patterns around a given medoid. The normality range is selected to minimize false positives (false identification of training samples from other patterns as a normal member of pattern that is being modeled) and false negatives (classification of normal samples of the pattern being modeled as anomalies). The algorithm for selection of customized normality range for each medoid, to enable multimodal m-Medoid based modeling of pattern, comprises of following steps:

1. Initialize significance parameter τ with the number of possible normality ranges for pattern c as computed in Step 2.
2. Sequentially input labeled training instances belonging to all classes and identify the closest medoid, indexed by r, using:

$$r = arg\ min_k\ dist(Q, M_k) \qquad \forall k \tag{8}$$

   where Q is the test sample.
3. Perform an anomaly test using the anomaly detection system, as proposed in section 4, assuming a one class classifier containing only pattern c represented by medoids set $\mathbf{M}^{(c)}$ using the current value of τ.
4. Increment false positive count $FP(r)$, corresponding to closest medoid M_r, each time when the sample is a normal member of pattern c but is identified as anomalous.

5. Increment false negative count $FN(r)$, corresponding to closest medoid M_r, each time when the sample is misclassified to pattern c.
6. Iterate through steps 2-5 for all the samples in DB.
7. Calculate Significance Parameter Validity Index $(SPVI)$ to check the effectiveness of current value of τ for a particular medoid using:

$$SPVI(k,\tau) = \beta \times FP(k) + (1-\beta) \times FN(k) \qquad 0 \leq \beta \leq 1 \quad \forall k \tag{9}$$

   where β is a scaling parameter to adjust the sensitivity of proposed classifier to false positives and false negatives according to specific requirements.
8. Set $\tau = \tau - 1$.
9. Iterate through step 2-8 till $\tau = 1$.
10. Identify the value of significance parameter for a given medoid as:

$$\underset{(c,k)}{\overbrace{\tau}} = arg\ min\ _{\tau} \quad SPVI(\tau,k) \quad \forall M_k \in \mathbf{M}^{(c)} \tag{10}$$

   where $\underset{(c,k)}{\overbrace{\tau}}$ is the dynamic significance parameter that have a different normality range for each medoid depending on the local density.

The space complexity of the proposed modeling algorithm in general feature space is $O(3 * n^2)$. The time complexity of our algorithm is the sum of time complexities of the three steps and is equivalent to $O(\omega * (n^2 + n^2 * log(n))) + O((\#_{medoids} * log(\#_{medoids}))) + O(|DB|^2 * \#_{medoids} * log(\#_{medoids}))$ where

- $O(n^2)$ is the time complexity of affinity matrix computation
- $O(n^2 * log(n))$ is the time complexity of message passing to compute availability and responsibility matrix
- ω is the number of times the modeling algorithm is repeated to identify m medoids. It has been observed that the value of ω normally lies in the range 3-10.
- $m * log(m)$ is the time complexity of computing possible normality range
- $|DB| * m$ is the time complexity for selecting customized normality range for each medoid where $|DB|$ is the number of trajectories present in trajectory dataset DB.

4. Classification and anomaly detection

Once the m-Medoids based model for all the classes have been learnt, the classification of new trajectories is performed by checking the closeness of said trajectory to the models of different classes. The classification of unseen samples to known classes and anomaly detection is performed using following steps:

1. Identify k nearest medoids, from the entire set of medoids $(\mathbf{M})$ belonging to different classes, to unseen sample Q as:

$$k\text{-NM}\ (Q, \mathbf{M}, k) = \{\mathbf{C} \in \mathbf{M} | \forall R \in \mathbf{C}, S \in \mathbf{M} - \mathbf{C}, \\ Dist(Q,R) \leq \text{Dist}(Q,S) \wedge |\mathbf{C}| = k\} \tag{11}$$

where $\mathbf{M}$ is the set of all medoids from different classes and $\mathbf{C}$ is the ordered set of k closest medoids starting from the nearest medoid.

2. Initialize nearest medoid index $\imath$ to 1.
3. Set r to the id of $\imath^{th}$ nearest medoid and c to the index of its corresponding class.
4. Set $l = \overbrace{\tau}_{(c,r)}$.
5. Identify the normality threshold d w.r.t. the medoid r using $\mathbf{D}^{(c)}$ as:

$$d = \mathbf{D}_l^{(c)} \tag{12}$$

6. Test sample Q is considered to be a valid member of class c if:

$$Dist(Q, M_r) \leq d \tag{13}$$

7. If the condition specified in eq. (13) is not satisfied, increment the index $\imath$ by 1.
8. Iterate steps 3-7 till $\imath$ gets equivalent to k. If the test trajectory Q has not been identified as a valid member of any class, it is considered to be an outlier and deemed anomalous.

The time complexity of MMC-GFS based classification and anomaly detection algorithm is $O(|\mathbf{M}|) + O(k)$ for anomalous samples where $|M|$ is the total number of medoids belonging to all classes. However, for most of the normal samples the time complexity is $O(|\mathbf{M}|)$. The time complexity can be further reduced by using efficient indexing structre like kd-trees to index $|\mathbf{M}|$ medoids for efficient k-NM search.

5. Relative merits of m-Medoids based modeling and classification algorithms

In this section, we provide a comparative evaluation of the proposed multimodal m-Medoids (MMC-GFS) and localized m-Medoids (Khalid, 2010a) based frameworks (LMC-ES) for modeling, classification and anomaly detection. These frameworks can be characterized in terms of the following attributes:

- Ability to deal with multimodal distribution within a pattern
- Ability to deal with variety of feature space representation of trajectories
- Time complexity of generating m-Medoids based model of known patterns
- Time complexity of classification and anomaly detection using learned models of normality
- Scalability of modeling mechanism to cope with increasing number of training data

For the ease in understanding of the comparative analysis, simulation of the working of proposed modeling and classification algorithms for arbitrary shaped patterns having multimodal distributions is presented in Fig. 1. In the left image of Fig. 1, each point represents the training sample and instances belonging to the same class are represented with same color and marker. Squares superimposed on each group of instances represent the medoids used for modeling the pattern. Normality region generated using different frameworks for classification and anomaly detection is depicted in the right image of Fig. 1. Test sample is considered to be a normal member of the class if it lies within the normality

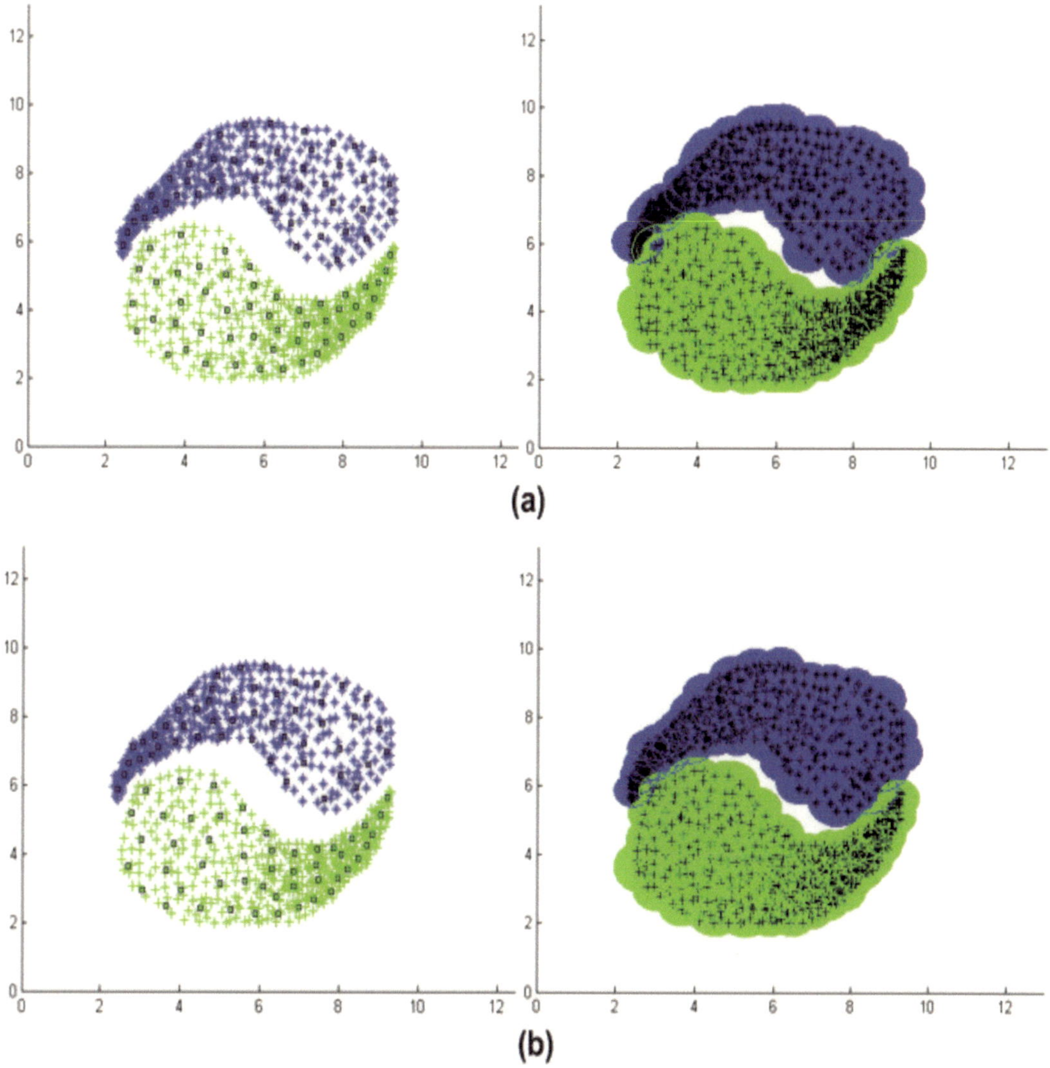

Fig. 1. m-Medoids based modeling of patterns using (a) LMC-ES framework (b) MMC-GFS framework.

region, else it is marked as anomalous. Visualization of LMC-ES and MMC-GFS based modeling is provided in Fig. 1(a) and Fig. 1(b) respectively.

Multimodal modeling using MMC-GFS frameworks caters for the multimodal distribution within a pattern. On the other hand, LMC-ES framework always assumes a unimodal distribution within a pattern and hence can not cater for the dynamic distribution of samples within a pattern. It is apparent from Fig. 1 that MMC-GFS frameworks have generated more accurate models that have accommodated the variation in sample density within a given pattern. LMC-ES framework performs a hard classification of unseen sample. A sample is classified to a pattern represented by the majority of medoids from a set of k nearest medoids. The sample may not lie in the normality region of a pattern to which it is classified and hence deemed anomalous. However, it is likely that it may still fall in the normality region of the second closest but less dense pattern having larger normality range. The hardness of LMC-ES based classification algorithm will result in the misclassification of such samples. However, MMC-GFS based classification and anomaly detection algorithm does not give a hard decision and checks for the membership of test trajectories w.r.t. different patterns until it is identified as a valid member of some pattern or it has been identified as anomalous w.r.t. k nearest medoids. This relatively softer approach enables the MMC-GFS based classification algorithm to adapt to the multimodal distribution of samples within different patterns. This phenomena is highlighted in Fig. 2. The samples, represented by 'x' marker, will be classified to blue pattern but is marked as anomalous using LMC-ES classifier as it falls outside the normality range of dense medoids belonging to the closest pattern. On the other hand, soft classification technique as proposed in MMC-GFS frameworks will correctly classify the sample as normal members of green pattern. Another benefit of MMC-GFS framework is that it can be applied to any feature space representation of trajectories with a given distance function. On the other hand, LMC-ES can only operate in feature spaces with a computable mean.

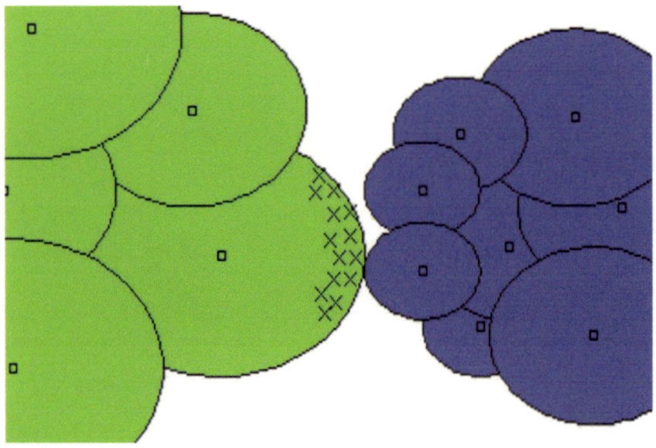

Fig. 2. Scenario for evaluating the adaptation of classification algorithms as proposed in different m-Medoids based frameworks.

Algorithms to generate m-Medoids model, as proposed in LMC-ES framework, is efficient and scalable to large datasets. On the other hand, the modeling algorithm of MMC-GFS is not scalable to very large datasets due to the requirement of affinity matrix computation. The space and time complexity is quadratic which is problematic for patterns with large number of training sample. However, this problem can be easily catered by splitting the training sample into subsets and selecting candidate medoids in each subset using algorithm as specified in section 3.1. The final selection of medoids can be done by applying the same algorithm again but now using the candidate medoids instead of all the training sample belonging to a given pattern. The classification algorithm of MMC-GFS framework is more efficient as compared to LMC-ES framework. This efficiency gain is due to the non-iterative unmerged anomaly detection with respect to a given medoid. The anomaly detection is done by applying a single threshold to the distance of the test sample from its $\imath^{th}$ closest medoid as specified in eq. (13). On the other hand, LMC-ES implements iterative merged anomaly detection, which is more accurate but time consuming as compared to the modeling algorithm proposed in MMC-GFS framework. The time complexity of merged anomaly detection is $O(m * log(m) - \tau * log(\tau))$.

6. Experimental results

In this section, we present some results to analyze the performance of the proposed multimodal m-Medoids based modeling, classification and anomaly detection as compared to competitive techniques.

6.1 Experimental datasets

Experiments are conducted on synthetic SIM_2 and real life LAB (Khalid, 2010a;b; Khalid & Naftel, 2006), HIGHWAY (Khalid & Naftel, 2006) and ASL (Bashir et al., 2006; 2005a;b; 2007; Khalid, 2010b; Khalid & Naftel, 2006) datasets. Details of these datasets can be found in Table 1.

Dataset	Description	# of trajectories	Extraction method	Labelled (Y/N)
SIM_2	Simulated dataset comprising of two dimensional coordinates.	arbitrary #	Simulation.	Y
LAB	Realistic dataset generated in the laboratory controlled environment for testing purposes. Trajectories can be categorised into 4 classes.	152	Tracking moving object and storing motion coordinates.	Y
HIGHWAY	Realistic vehicle trajectory dataset generated by tracking vehicles in a highway traffic surveillance sequence.	355	Tracking vehicles using PTMS(Melo et al., 2004) tracking algorithm.	Y
ASL	Trajectories of right hand of signers as different words are signed. Dataset consists of signs for 95 different word classes with 70 samples per word.	6650	Extracting (x, y) coordinates of the mass of right hand from files containing complete sign information.	Y

Table 1. Overview of datasets used for experimental evaluation

6.2 Experiment 1: Evaluation of m-Medoids based frameworks for classification and anomaly detection

The purpose of this experiment is to evaluate the performance of proposed MMC-GFS and LMC-ES based frameworks for classification of unseen data samples to one of the known patterns. The effectiveness of the proposed frameworks to perform anomaly detection is also demonstrated here. The experiment has been conducted on simulated SIM_2 dataset. Training

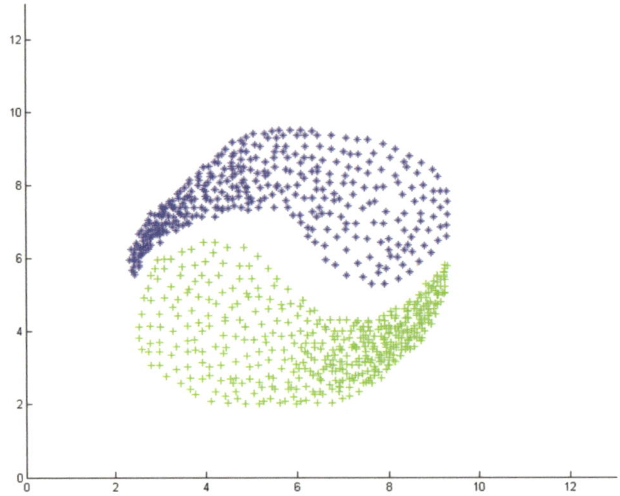

Fig. 3. Training data from SIM_2 dataset.

data from simulated datasets is shown in Fig. 3. Test data for SIM_2 dataset is obtained by generating 500 samples from a uniform distribution such that $(x, y) \in (U(1, 12), U(1, 12))$.

We have used 50 medoids to model a class using its member samples. The classification and anomaly detection results for SIM_2 dataset, using LMC-ES and MMC-GFS frameworks are presented in Fig. 4(a) and Fig. 4(b) respectively. Training samples are represented using '+' marker whereas classified normal samples are represented by small circles. Data points belonging to same class are represented with same colour and marker. Samples from test data which have been identified as anomalous are represented with a black 'x' marker. It is apparent from Fig. 4 that multimodal m-Medoids based classification system as proposed in MMC-GFS framework performs better classification and anomaly detection while catering for multimodal distribution within the modeled pattern. On the other hand, LMC-ES based framework performs unimodal modeling of patterns and therefore the classification system does not adjust well to the variation of density within a pattern.

After demonstrating the efficacy of proposed classification and anomaly detection approach on synthetic data, the experiment is then repeated on real life LAB and HIGHWAY datasets. LAB and HIGHWAY datasets are classified motion datasets and contain anomalous trajectories within the datasets themselves. Classified training data for these datasets is obtained by randomly selecting half of the trajectories from each of the normal patterns in the dataset. The remaining half of the trajectories from the normal patterns along with anomalous trajectories are extracted and used as test data. Training samples from the LAB and HIGHWAY datasets are shown in Fig. 5 and Fig. 6 respectively. For ease of visualization, samples from each class are plotted separately on the background scene. The starting point of each trajectory is marked in green.

Trajectories from LAB and HIGHWAY datasets are modelled using DFT-MOD based coefficient feature vectors. (Khalid, 2010b). Patterns are modeled using 20 medoids per pattern. Once the multimodal m-Medoids based model for all the classes have been learnt, classification of samples from the test data is done using the classifier as proposed in section

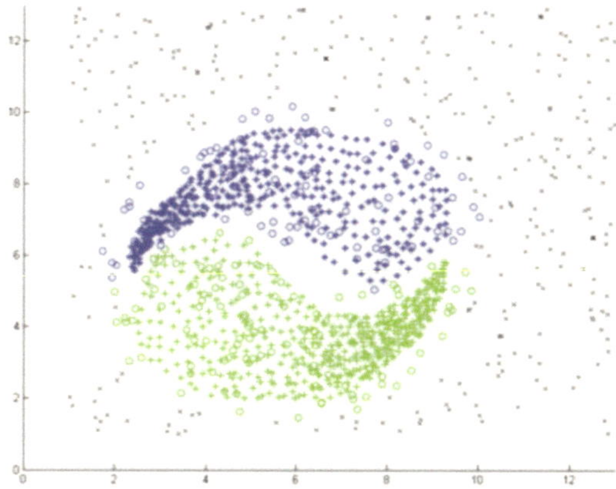

(a)

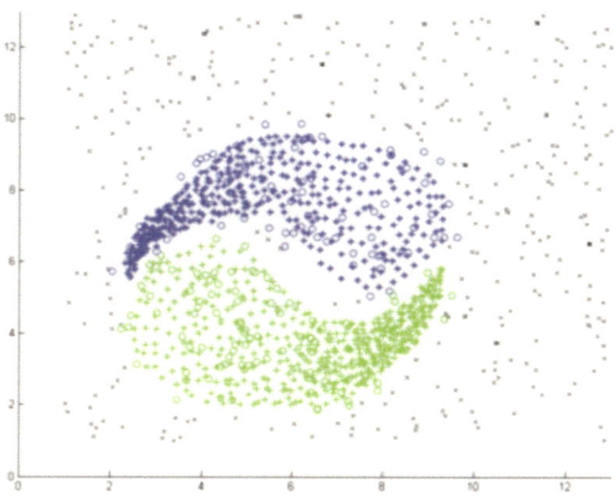

(b)

Fig. 4. Classification of test data, based on SIM_2 classes, using (a) LMC-ES framework (b) MMC-GFS framework.

4. Classification obtained by applying the MMC-GFS approach on LAB dataset is shown in Fig. 7. The matching of classification obtained for each trajectory with its ground truth shows that no trajectory is misclassified. Trajectories identified as anomalous are shown in Fig. 8. It is clear from Fig. 8 that anomalous trajectories are significantly different from the normal motion patterns as shown in Fig. 7. The classification experiment is also conducted on the HIGHWAY dataset and the results obtained are shown in Fig. 9. Trajectories filtered as anomalous are shown in Fig. 10. These experimental results give evidence to the claim that MMC-GFS based classification and anomaly detection system is an effective and robust approach that works well with real life motion datasets.

6.3 Experiment 2: Comparison of proposed classifiers with competitive techniques

The purpose of this experiment is to compare the performance of classifiers as proposed in LMC-ES and MMC-GFS frameworks. For comparison of our results with competitive techniques, we establish a base case by implementing three different systems for comparison including Mahalanobis and GMM classifier. Real life ASL dataset is used for the experiment.

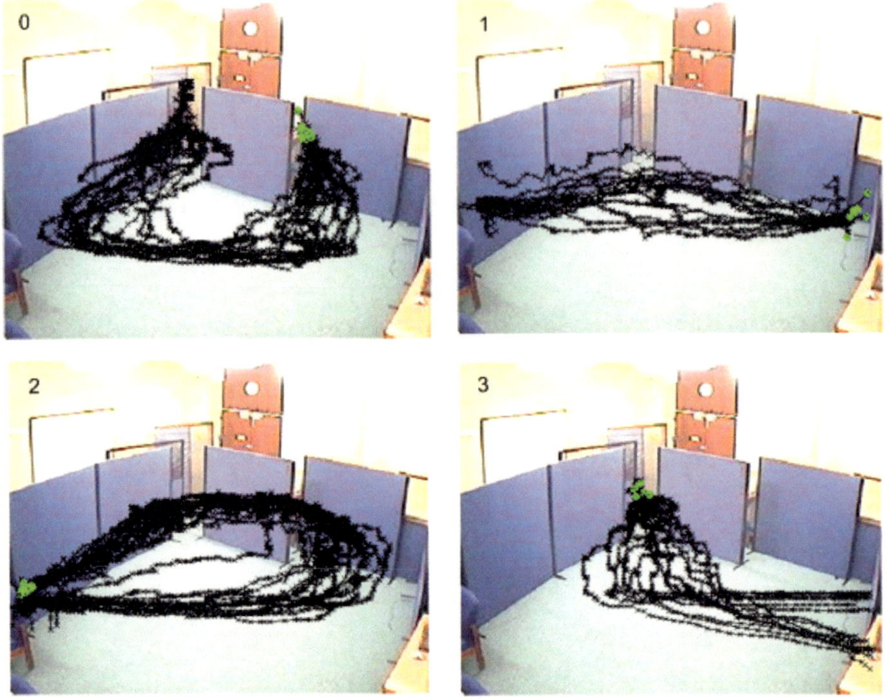

Fig. 5. Labelled training samples from LAB dataset. Trajectories belonging to different classes are plotted separately on background scene

Signs from different number of word classes are selected. Classified training data is obtained by randomly selecting half of the trajectories from each word class leaving the other half to be used as test data. Trajectories from ASL dataset are represented using DFT-MOD based coefficient feature vectors (Khalid, 2010b). Patterns are modeled using 20 medoids per pattern. We have computed single multimodal Gaussian for modeling of patterns for Mahalanobis classifier. Modeling of patterns and classification of unseen samples using GMM is based on the approach as described in (Bashir et al., 2005a). Each class is modeled using a separate GMM. The number of modes to be used for GMM-based modeling is automatically estimated using a string of pruning, merging and mode-splitting processes as specified in (Bashir et al., 2005a). Once the models for all the classes have been learnt, the test data is passed to different classifiers and the class labels obtained are compared with the ground truth. The experiment is repeated with different numbers and combinations of word classes. Each classification experiment is averaged over 50 runs to reduce any bias resulting from favorable word selection.

The accuracy of different classifiers for wide range of word classes from ASL dataset is presented in Table 2. Based on these results, we can see that the multimodal m-Medoids based classifier as proposed in MMC-GFS framework yield a superior classification accuracy as compared to other classifiers closely followed by unimodal LMC-ES framework. GMM yields good results for lower number of classes but its performance deteriorates for higher number of word classes. It can also be observed from Table 2 that the relative accuracy of proposed m-Medoids based MMC-GFS and LMC-ES classifiers increases with an increase in the number

Fig. 6. Labelled training samples from HIGHWAY dataset. Trajectories belonging to different classes are plotted separately on background scene

	ASL (#classes : #samples)				
	2 : 70	**4 : 140**	**8 : 280**	**16 : 560**	**24:840**
MMC-GFS	0.99	0.94	0.91	0.86	0.83
LMC-ES	0.98	0.92	0.88	0.83	0.78
Mahalanobis	0.95	0.88	0.82	0.75	0.71
GMM	0.97	0.92	0.83	0.74	0.69

Table 2. Classification accuracies for different number of classes from ASL dataset

of classes as compared with competitive techniques; thus making them more scalable for larger number of classes. The superior performance of MMC-GFS, as compared to competitive techniques, can be explained by the fact that the proposed multimodal m-Medoids based frameworks do not impose any restriction on the probability distribution function of modeled patterns. The proposed frameworks can effectively model arbitrary shaped patterns and can effectively handle variation in sample distribution within a pattern as demonstrated in Fig. 1 and Fig. 4. On the other hand, the competitive approaches impose assumptions on the PDF of patterns (normally gaussian). These approaches do not have the capacity to handle multimodal distribution within a pattern. As a result, the model generated by these approaches will not give an accurate representation of complex patterns and hence result in poor classification performance as compared to the proposed multimodal m-Medoids based approaches.

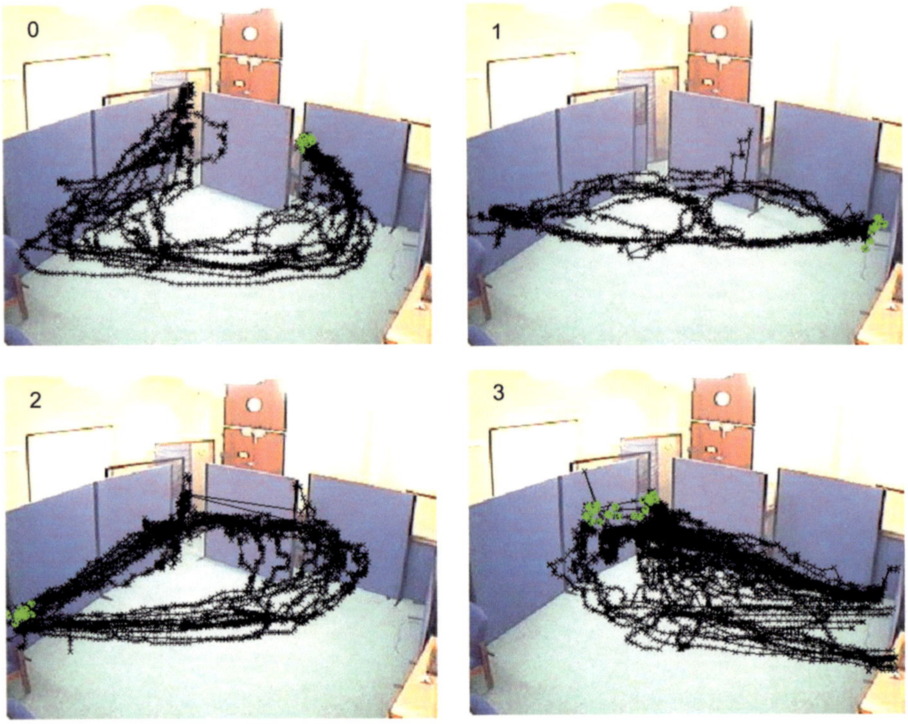

Fig. 7. Classification of test trajectories from LAB dataset

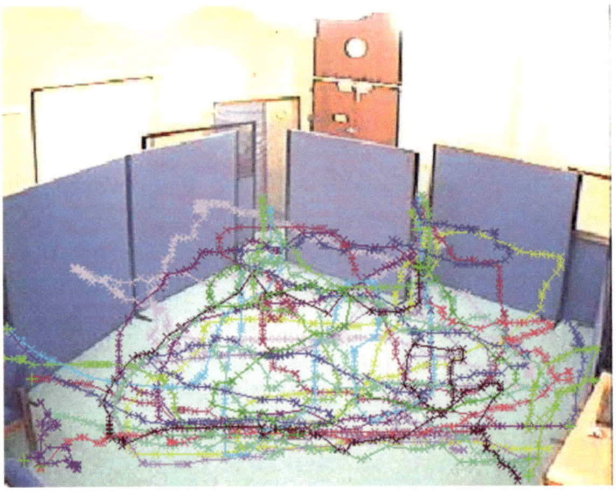

Fig. 8. Trajectories identified as anomalous from LAB dataset using proposed anomaly detection mechanism.

Fig. 9. Classification of test trajectories from HIGHWAY dataset

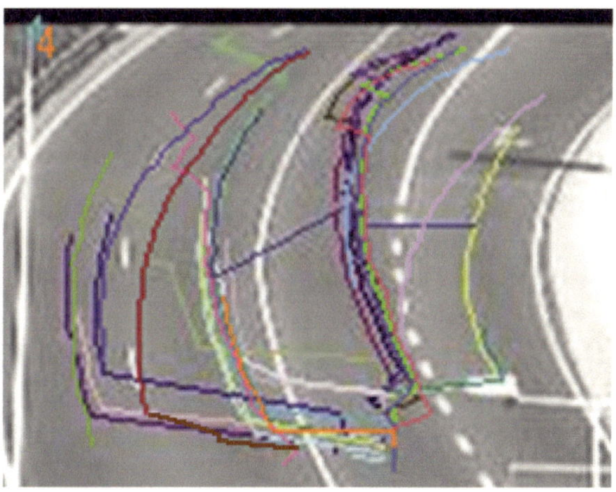

Fig. 10. Trajectories identified as anomalous from HIGHWAY dataset using proposed anomaly detection mechanism.

Similar experiment with ASL dataset (using similar experimental settings) has been conducted by (Bashir et al., 2007) using their proposed GMM and HMM-based classification system. They reported classification accuracies of 0.96, 0.92, 0.86 and 0.78 for 2, 4, 8 and 16 word classes respectively. A comparison of these classification accuracies with the results obtained using our approach reveals that classifiers from *m*-Medoids classifier family performs better than GMM and HMM-based recognition system (Bashir et al., 2007) despite the fact that our proposed classification approach is conceptually simpler and computationally less expensive.

6.4 Experiment 3: Quantitative evaluation of anomaly detection algorithms

Here we provide a quantitative evaluation and comparison of *m*-Medoids based anomaly detection algorithms, as proposed in MMC-GFS and LMC-ES frameworks, with competitors. We implemented three different anomaly detection techniques based on statistical test as proposed in (Khalid & Naftel, 2006), Grown When Required (GWR) novelty filter as proposed in (Marsland et al., 2002) and one-class classifier based anomaly detection as proposed in (Tax, 2001). (Khalid & Naftel, 2006) performs anomaly detection by using Mahalanobis classifier and conducting Hotelling's T^2 test. (Tax, 2001) perform anomaly detection by generating model of one class (referred to as target class) and distinguishing it from samples belonging to all other classes. There generation of model of the target class is done using SVM and GMM. For SVM-based one class classifier (OCC-SVM), we have used RBF kernel for the modeing of target class. For GMM-based one class classifier (OCC-GMM), we have used the approach as specified in Experiment 2 to generate the GMM-based model.

The experiment has been conducted using different number of word classes from ASL dataset. We have extracted half of the samples belonging to each word class for training purposes leaving the other half of the samples to be used as test data. DFT-MOD based coefficient feature vector representation of sign trajectories from training data is generated and used to generate models as required by the different classification approaches. MMC-GFS and LMC-ES framework based model of each class is generated using the algorithm as presented in section 3 and (Khalid, 2010a) respectively. Patterns are modeled using 20 medoids per pattern.

Once the model learning phase is over, anomaly detection using different techniques is carried out using test dataset. We would expect that few instances drawn from class X would be recorded as anomalous when tested against the same class, whereas nearly all instances would be detected as anomalous when tested against a different class Y. The experiment is repeated with different numbers and combinations of word classes. Each anomaly detection experiment is averaged over 50 runs to reduce any bias resulting from favorable word selection.

Fig. 11 reports the result in terms of percentage of correct anomaly detection using various number of word classes from ASL dataset. The results demonstrate the superiority of anomaly detection using *m*-Medoids based MMC-GFS and LMC-ES frameworks. The anomaly detection accuracies obtained using MMC-GFS algorith are higher than unimodal LMC-ES based anomaly detection algorithm. MMC-GFS and LMC-ES performs better than OCC-SVM, OCC-GMM, GWR and Mahalanobis framework-based Naftel's method. The superior performance of proposed approach as compared to state-of-the-art techniques is due to the fact that our approach gives importance to correct classification of normal sample and to the filtration of abnormal samples during the model generation phase. On the other hand, OCC-SVM generates good model of normal classes but classifies many of the abnormal samples as member of normal classes whereas GWR gives extra importance to filtering abnormal samples and in the process, identifies many normal samples as abnormal.

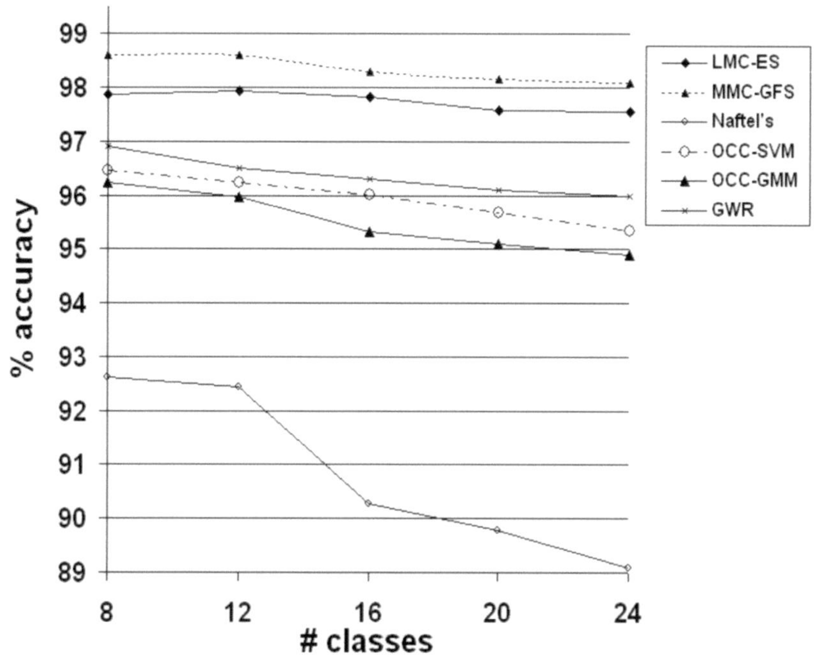

Fig. 11. Percentage anomaly detection accuracies for different number of classes from ASL dataset

7. Discussion and conclusions

In this chapter, we have presented an extended *m*-Medoids based framework, referred to as MMC-GFS, for modeling of trajectory-based motion patterns. The strength of the proposed approach is its ability to model complex patterns without imposing any restriction on the distribution of samples within a given pattern. Once the multimodal *m*-Medoids model for all the classes have been learnt, the classification of new trajectories and anomaly detection is then performed using a proposed soft classification and anomaly detection algorithm which is adaptive to multimodal distributions of samples within a pattern. The strength of this technique is its ability to model complex patterns without imposing any restriction on the shape of patterns. MMC-GFS can be used for modeling, classification and anomaly detection in any feature space with a computable similarity function.

Experimental results are presented to show the effectiveness of proposed MMC-GFS classifier. Modeling of pattern and classification using proposed frameworks is unaffected by variation of sample distribution within a pattern as demonstrated in Fig. 4. Quantitative comparison of MMC-GFS based classifiers with competitive techniques demonstrates the superiority of our multimodal approach as it performs consistently better than commonly used Mahalanobis, GMM and HMM-based classifiers.

Experiments are also conducted to show the effectiveness of anomaly detection capabilities of proposed frameworks. Anomaly detection results for different classes of ASL datasets, using different variants of proposed anomaly detection algorithm, are presented. It has been shown that anomaly detection using multimodal MMC-GFS frameworks gives better anomaly detection accuracies as compared to the unimodal LMC-ES approach. Although LMC-ES enables the anomaly detection system to adapt to the normality distribution of individual classes, it is insensitive to the variation of distributions within a pattern which results in degradation of its performance as compared to MMC-GFS frameworks. Comparison of proposed anomaly detection algorithms with an existing approach demonstrates the superiority of our approach approach as they consistently perform better for different number of classes.

The application of proposed MMC-GFS based modeling and recognition system is not only limited to trajectory-based behavior recognition, but can also be applied to other recognition tasks that are critical in video surveillance application. Some of the applications where MMC-GFS based modeling and classification system can be applied include but is not limited to object recognition in surveillance videos, gait recognition, scene recognition etc.

8. References

Aghbari, Z., Kaneko, K. & Makinouchi, A. (2003). Content-trajectory approach for searching video databases, *IEEE Transanction on Multimedia*, Vol. 5 of 4, pp. 516–531.

Bashir, F. I., Khokhar, A. A. & Schonfeld, D. (2006). View-invariant motion trajectory based activity classification and recognition, *ACM Multimedia Systems, special issue on Machine Learning Approaches to Multimedia Information retrieval*, pp. 45–54.

Bashir, F. I., Khokhar, A. A. & Schonfield, D. (2003). Segmented trajectory based indexing and retrieval of video data, *IEEE International Conference on Image Processing*, Vol. 3, Barcelona, Spain, pp. II– 623–6.

Bashir, F. I., Khokhar, A. A. & Schonfield, D. (2004). A hybrid system for affine-invariant trajectory retrieval, *Proc. MIR'04*, pp. 235–242.

Bashir, F. I., Khokhar, A. A. & Schonfield, D. (2005a). Automatic object trajectory based motion recognition using gaussian mixture models, *IEEE International Conference on Multimedia and Expo*, Netherland, pp. 1532– 1535.

Bashir, F. I., Khokhar, A. A. & Schonfield, D. (2005b). Hmm based motion recognition system using segmented pca, *IEEE International Conference on Image Processing*, Genova, Italy, pp. 1288–1291.

Bashir, F. I., Khokhar, A. A. & Schonfield, D. (2007). Object trajectory-based activity classification and recognition using hidden markov models, *IEEE Transactions on Image Processing*, Vol. 16 of 7, pp. 1912–1919.

Brotherton, T., Johnson, T. & Chadderdon, G. (1998). Classification and novelty detection using linear models and a class dependent elliptical basis function neural network, *Proc. IJCNN Conference*, Vol. 2, Anchorage, pp. 876–879.

Cai, Y. & Ng, R. (2004). Indexing spatio-temporal trajectories with chebyshev polynomials, *ACM SIGMOD/PODS Conference*, France, pp. 599–610.

Chan, K. & Fu, A. (1999). Efficient time series matching by wavelets, *Proc. of International Conference on Data Engineering*, Sydney, pp. 126–133.

Chang, S. F., Chen, W., Horace, J. M., Sundaram, H. & Zhong, D. (1998). A fully automated content based video search engine supporting spatiotemporal queries, *IEEE Transactions on Circuits and System for Video Technology*, Vol. 8 of *5*, pp. 602–615.

Dagtas, S., Ali-Khatib, W., Ghafor, A. & Kashyap, R. (2000). Models for motion-based video indexing and retrieval, *IEEE Transactions on Image Processing*, Vol. 9 of *1*, pp. 88–101.

Faloutsos, C., Ranganathan, M. & Manolopoulos, Y. (1994). Fast sub-sequence matching in time-series databases, *Proceedings of the 1994 ACM SIGMOD International Conference on Management of Data*, pp. 419–429.

Frey, B. & Dueck, D. (2007). Science, Vol. 315, pp. 972–976.

Hamid, R., Johnson, A., Batta, S., Bobick, A., Isbell, C. & Coleman, G. (2005). Detection and explanation of anomalous activities: Representing activities as bags of events n-grams., *CVPR*, pp. 1031–1038.

Hsu, C.-T. & Teng, S.-J. (2002). Motion trajectory based video indexing and retrieval, *IEEE International Conference on Image Processing*, Vol. 1, pp. 605–608.

Hu, W., Tan, T., Wang, L. & Maybank, S. (2004). A survey on visual surveillance of object motion and behaviors, *IEEE Transactions on Systems, Man & Cybernetic*, Vol. 34 of *3*, pp. 334–352.

Hu, W., Xiao, X., Fu, Z., Xie, D., Tan, T. & Maybank, S. (2006). A system for learning statistical motion patterns, *IEEE Transactions on Pattern Analysis and Machine Learning*, Vol. 28 of *9*, pp. 1450–1464.

Hu, W., Xiao, X., Xie, D., Tan, T. & Maybank, S. (2004). Traffic accident prediction using 3-d model based vehicle tracking, *IEEE Transactions on Vehicular Tech*, Vol. 53 of *3*, pp. 677–694.

Hu, W., Xie, D., Fu, Z., Zeng, W. & Maybank, S. (2007). Semantic based surveillance video retrieval, *IEEE Transactions on ImageProcessing*, pp. 1168–1181.

Hu, W., Xie, D., Tan, T. & Maybank, S. (2004). Learning activity patterns using fuzzy self-organizing neural networks, *IEEE Transactions on Systems, Man & Cybernetic*, Vol. 34 of *3*, pp. 1618–1626.

Jeanin, S. & Divakaran, A. (2001). Mpeg-7 visual motion descriptors, *IEEE Trans. Circuits Syst. Video Technol.*, Vol. 11 of *6*, pp. 720–724.

Jin, Y. & Mokhtarian, F. (2004). Efficient video retrieval by motion trajectory, *Proceedings of British Machine Vision Conference*, Kingston, pp. 667–676.

Johnson, N. & Hogg, D. (1995). Learning the distribution of object trajectories for event recognition, *Proceedings of British Conference on Machine Vision*, pp. 582–592.

Keogh, E., Chakrabarti, K., Pazzani, M. & Mehrota, S. (2001). Locally adaptive dimensionality reduction for indexing large time series databases, *Proc. ACM SIGMOD Conference*, pp. 151–162.

Khalid, S. (2010a). Activity classification and anomaly detection using m-mediods based modeling of motion patterns, *Pattern Recognition*, Vol. 43, pp. 3636–3647.

Khalid, S. (2010b). Motion based behaviour learning, profiling and classification in the presence on anomalies, *Pattern Recognition*, Vol. 43, pp. 173–186.

Khalid, S. & Naftel, A. (2005). Evaluation of matching metrics for trajectory based indexing and retrieval of video clips, *Proceedings of IEEE WACV*, Colorado, USA, pp. 242–249.

Khalid, S. & Naftel, A. (2006). Classifying spatiotemporal object trajectories using unsupervised learning in the coefficient feature space, *Multimedia Systems*, Vol. 12, pp. 227–238.

Marsland, S., Shapiro, J. & Nehmzow, U. (2002). A self-organising network that grows when required, *Neural Networks*, Vol. 15, pp. 1041–1058.

Melo, J., Naftel, A., Bernardino, A. & Santos-Victor, J. (2004). Viewpoint independent detection of vehicle trajectories and lane geometry from uncalibrated traffic surveilllance cameras, *Proc. of International Confernce of Image Analysis and Recognition*, Porto, Portugal, pp. 454–462.

Owens, J. & Hunter, A. (2000). Application of the self-organising map for trajectory classification, *Proceedings of Third IEEE International Workshop on Visual Surveillance*, Dublin, Ireland, p. 77.

Rea, N., Dahyot, R. & Kokaram, A. (2004). Semantic event detection in sports through motion understanding, *Proceedings of Conference on Image and Video Retrieval*, Dublin, Ireland, pp. 88–97.

Roberts, S. & Tarassenko, L. (1994). A probabilistic resource allocating network for novelty detection, *Neural Computation*, Vol. 6, pp. 270–284.

Shim, C. & Chang, J. (2001). Content based retrieval using trajectories of moving objects in video databases, *Proceedings of IEEE 7th International Conference on Database Systems for Advanced Applications*, pp. 169–170.

Shim, C. & Chang, J. (2004). Trajectory based video retrieval for multimedia information systems, *Proceedings of ADVIS*, pp. 372–382.

Tax, D. (2001). One-class classification, *PhD thesis, Delft University of Technology*.

Vlachos, M., Kollios, G. & Gunopulos, D. (2002). Discovering similar multidimensional trajectories, *Proceedings of the International Conference on Data Engineering*, San Jose, CA, pp. 673–684.

Xiang, T. & Gong, S. (2005). Video behaviour profiling and abnormality detection without manual labelling, *Proc. IEEE International Conference on Computer Vision*, Vol. 2, London, UK, pp. 1238– 1245.

Xiang, T. & Gong, S. (2006). Incremental visual behaviour modelling, *The 6th IEEE Workshop on Visual Surveillance*, Graz, pp. 65–72.

Yacoob, Y. & Black, M. (1999). Parameterized modeling and recognition of activities, *Computer Vision and Image Understanding*, Vol. 73, pp. 232–247.

Yeung, D. & Chow, C. (2002). Parzen window network intrusion detectors, *Proc. International Conference on Pattern Recognition, IEEE*, Canada, pp. 385–388.

Zhang, D., Gatica-Perez, Bengio, S. & McCowan, I. (2005). Semi-supervised adapted hmms for unusual event detection, *Proceedings of IEEE International Conference on Computer Vision and Pattern Recognition*, pp. 611–618.

Zhong, H., Shi, J. & Visontai, M. (2004). Detecting unusual activity in videos, *Proc. Of CVPR*, Washington D.C., pp. 819–826.